THE WIND GOURD OF LA'AMAOMAO

Revised Edition, 2005

THE WIND GOURD OF LA'AMAOMAO

The Hawaiian Story
of
Pāka'a and Kūapāka'a

Personal Attendants of Keawenuia'umi
Ruling Chief of Hawaii
and
Descendants of La'amaomao

BY

MOSES KUAEA NAKUINA

TRANSLATED
BY
ESTHER T. MOOKINI AND SARAH NĀKOA

KALAMAKŪ PRESS
Revised Edition, 2005

ISBN-13: 9781519641632
ISBN-10: 151964163X

Kalamakū Press
1710 Punahou Street, Apt. 601
Honolulu, HI 96822

The Wind Gourd of La'amaomao, Revised Edition, 2005. Earlier versions were published in 1990, 1992, 1996, 1999.

Printed in the United States of America

Cover art and design by 'Elepaio Press

Contents

INTRODUCTION

The Wind Gourd of La'amaomao is a translation of *Moolelo Hawaii o Pakaa a me Ku-a-Pakaa, na Kahu Iwikuamoo o Keawenuiaumi, ke Alii o Hawaii, a o na Moopuna hoi a Laamaomao* ("The Hawaiian Story of Pakaa and Ku-a-Pakaa, the Personal Attendants of Keawenuiaumi, the Chief of Hawaii, and the Descendants of Laamaomao"), a traditional legend collected from various sources, edited, and expanded by Moses Kuaea Nakuina, and published in 1902. In his preface, addressed to "those who truly love the Ali'i and the Lahui [Hawaiian Nation]," Nakuina says he felt great mana (power) in the book and explains its value: "First, it is written in the authentic Hawaiian language as it was heard in the past. Second, some songs, improvised chants, and sacred chants have been forgotten, and others will soon be forgotten; we will never remember them if books such as this one are not published. Third, the book contains the names of the winds of all the Hawaiian Islands, known as the Territory of Hawaii today. Fourth, and most importantly, the book expresses the sincere love for the Ali'i the kānaka of Hawai'i felt in the past and still feel today." Nine years after the overthrow of the Hawaiian Monarchy in 1893 by Americans, Nakuina was calling on his Hawaiian readers to remember their true leaders, nation, and culture: "Here are Pāka'a and Kūapāka'a searching for all of you; recognize them if they peep in at your doors, and call out and welcome them into your homes."

Set mainly on Hawai'i, Kaua'i, and Moloka'i, the story concerns the close relationship between the ali'i and his kahu iwikuamo'o, or personal attendant, and their responsibilities to each other and the people they ruled. The story portrays the ideal attendant as one who was caring and just toward both his ali'i and the maka'āinana, or commoners. Ancestry was essential in establishing status and access to privileges and special powers (such as control over the winds); but also important was the ability to carry out efficiently and fairly the duties of leadership.

Judging from its extensive development and the number of versions recorded in Hawaiian after Hawaiians adopted the haole writing system in the 19th century, the story seems to have been highly regarded both for its artistry and for promoting such values as honesty, generosity, loyalty, filial piety, and justice (which included vengeance). The first known publication of the legend in Hawaiian is a rendition by S.K. Kuapuu simply entitled *He Wahi Moolelo*, which appeared serially in the Hawaiian newspaper *Ka Hae Hawaii* from April 17–June 19, 1861. A version by S.M. Kamakau entitled *He Moolelo no Pakaa* ("The Story of Pakaa") appeared serially in the Hawaiian newspapers *Ke Au Okoa* and *Ka Nupepa Kuokoa* from 1869-1871. Another Hawaiian text of the Pākaʻa story appears in Fornander's *Hawaiian Antiquities and Folk-lore* (Vol. 4, 72-135). This rendition, accompanied by an English translation, does not contain all of the incidents and chants that appear in Nakuina's, but the two stories are similar and some of the chants are identical. Nakuina seems to have used all three of these earlier Hawaiian texts as sources for his expanded version.

English renditions of the story include a long version in William Hyde Rice's collection *Hawaiian Legends* (1923); a short version in Thomas G. Thrum's collection *More Hawaiian Folktales* (1923); a short, young adult's version in Cora Wells Thorpe's *In the Path of the Trade Winds* (1924); a short children's version in Mary Kawena Pukui and Caroline Curtis' collection *The Water of Kane* (1951); and most recently, a book-length young adult's version by Marcia Brown entitled *The Backbone of the King* (1966), which is based on a translation of Nakuina's text by Dorothy Kahananui. Of the English versions, Rice's most closely resembles Nakuina's in its completeness of plot, although Rice summarizes or omits the chants, which are important elements in the artistry and plot of the story. According to the introduction to his collection, Rice heard the story from "a man from Hawaiʻi named Wiu," but Nakuina's story may have been the original source. This present text, unlike earlier English versions, is a complete translation rather than a simplification or summary.

The wind gourd referred to in the title of this legend was believed to contain all the winds of Hawaiʻi, which could be called forth by chanting their names. According to Handy and Handy, the gourd is an embodiment of Lono, the Hawaiian god of agriculture and fertility: "Lono is the gourd; the cosmic gourd is the heavens whence come winds, clouds, and rain" (220). In the Pākaʻa legend, the gourd, along with the marvelous wind chants naming dozens of local winds, is passed down from Laʻamaomao, the Hawaiian wind goddess (lit. "distant sacredness"), to her granddaughter Laʻamaomao; to her granddaughter's son Pākaʻa; to Pākaʻa's son, Kū-a-Pākaʻa. In "The Triple Marriage of Laa-Mai-Kahiki" (Kalākaua, *The Legends and Myths of Hawaii*), Laʻamaomao is described as a god rather than a goddess. He accompanies Moikeha to Hawai'i from Kahiki and settles at Hale-o-Lono on the island of Moloka'i, where he was worshiped as an 'aumakua, or deity, of the winds. The female gender of the wind deity in the Pāka'a story seems to be a Hawaiian development as the wind deity in other Polynesian traditions is male (Ra'a—Society Islands, Raka—Cook Islands, Raka-maomao—New Zealand).

In Mangaia, in the Cook Islands, a gourd representing the heavenly dome was also used in traditional times to control the winds: "…the high priest possessed a magic calabash, a miniature universe, which had holes bored in a circle at equal distances around its middle, representing the openings on the horizon through which the thirty-two winds of the compass were supposed to blow. When a voyage was contemplated to a distant island the priest was induced to stop up all the holes in the calabash except the one at the particular point of the compass from which the prospective travelers desired the wind to blow for the speedy consummation of the voyage" (Makemson 147). Lewis quotes Gill about the importance of knowledge of the winds: "'In olden times, great stress was laid on this knowledge for the purpose of fishing, and especially for their long sea voyages from group to group. At the edge of the horizon are a series of holes … through which Raka, the god of winds, and his children, love to blow…'" (75).

In the Bishop Museum collection is a gourd named the wind gourd of La'amaomao. Its inscription reads: "The wind gourd of Laamaomao that was in the keeping of Hauna, personal attendant of Lonoikamakahiki I [Keawenuia'umi's youngest son]. It was passed on to Pakaa, a personal attendant of Keawenuiaumi. It was placed in the royal burial cave of Hoaiku on the sacred cliffs of Keoua, at Kaawaloa, island of Hawaii, and received by King Kalakaua I on January 1, 1883, from Kaapana, caretaker of Hoaiku." The gourd was donated to the museum by Princess Kalaniana'ole in 1923.

Dennis Kawaharada
Honolulu, 1992

ix

MOSES KUAEA NAKUINA

Moses Kuaea Nakuina (born July 12, 1867, in Waialua, Oʻahu) was the first president of the Christian Endeavor Union in Hawaiʻi (1903), a member of the Territorial House of Representatives (elected from Maui, Molokaʻi, and Lānaʻi in 1904), and editor of the Hawaiian newspaper Ka Hoaloha (1907). His parents were John and Kaimawaho Nakuina, who were married on Maui; he was the grandson of Puakaloheau, the great-grandson of Kekaiakea, and the nephew of Reverend Kuaea of Kaumakapili Church in Honolulu. Nakuina attended Royal School in Honolulu. He went to the boarding school in Malumalu, Kauaʻi, when his father became a county judge in Hanalei. When his father was sent to teach in Hilo, Nakuina attended Hilo Boarding School. Later he continued his education at Royal School on Oʻahu.

After his father's death, Nakuina went to work at the Government Records Office in Honolulu to support himself and his mother. The office was administered by Emma M. Beckley, a part-Hawaiian woman who was a commissioner of water rights, an authority on Hawaiian culture, and the first curator of Hawaiʻi's National Museum, as well as an author and storyteller. Moses married Emma (the widow of part-Hawaiian Fred K. Beckley) in 1887, the year he began working in the Records Office. In addition to serving in positions of business, government, and the church, Nakuina collected and published Hawaiian folktales and wrote and translated articles on Hawaiian culture. He spent the last years of his life as a minister of Kaumakapili Church, working strenuously with the prohibition campaign in 1910. He died at the age of 44 on August 3, 1911 at his Kaimukī home. In 1915, a bronze tablet in his memory was placed in Kaumakapili Church by the Christian Endeavor Societies.

In addition to Moolelo Hawaii o Pakaa a me Ku-a-Pakaa (The Hawaiian Story of Pakaa and Ku-a-Pakaa), Nakuina also published an incomplete story entitled Moolelo Hawaii o Kalapana, ke keiki hoopapa o Puna (The Hawaiian Story of Kalapana, a native-born child of Puna) in 1902. His articles and English translations of Hawaiian articles by other writers appeared in Thrum's Hawaiian Annual and include "Stories of Menehunes" (1895), "Hawaiian Surf Riding" (1896), "Fish Stories and Superstitions" (1901), "Ku-ula, the Fish God of Hawaiʻi" (1901), and "Aiai, Son of Ku-ula" (1902).

THE TRANSLATORS

Esther T. Mookini is a retired Hawaiian language and history instructor. Her publications include *O na Holoholona Wawae Eha o Ka Lama Hawaii/The Four-Footed Animals of Ka Lama Hawaii*, 1985) and The Hawaiian Newspapers (1974). She is also co-translator with Erin C. Neizmen of *He Moolelo no Kamapuaa/The Story of Kamapuaa* (1978) and co-compiler of *Place Names of Hawaii* (1974), The Pocket Hawaiian Dictionary (1975), and *Pocket Place Names of Hawaii* (1989).

Sarah Nākoa (1911-1990) taught Hawaiian Language at the University of Hawai'i at Mānoa and Kamehameha Schools and was a translator for the Hawai'i State Archives. She is the author of *Lei Momi o 'Ewa* (1979), a collection of stories about her home district of 'Ewa.

TRANSLATOR'S NOTE

Sarah Nākoa and I decided to translate the Pāka'a legend in the summer of 1985, and for five years she worked closely with me. She passed away soon after the translation was completed in 1990.

Aunty Sarah had a deep and intimate knowledge of the Hawaiian language, Hawaiian values, and the Hawaiian way of life and gave meaning to many words, phrases, and lines which are esoteric today. The chants in the Pāka'a story were especially problematic. They are full of puns, riddles, allusions, and archaic words that make them difficult for the modern translator to understand and render into English. The translations of the chants in the Fornander collection have been used as guides and adopted in places.

My teacher and friend Ruby Kawena Johnson also helped clarify some difficult passages containing puns and riddles. She has graciously answered my calls for help and has given her knowledge unselfishly. Mahalo au iā 'oe, e Kawena.

Richard Hamasaki and Kīhei de Silva read the translation carefully and made important and insightful comments.

John Charlot has been a steady supporter. For allowing me to read his collection of information on Nakuina, my deep gratitude. To his student Leinaala Simmons, thank you for doing the initial research on Nakuina and for allowing us to use it in this work.

Ruth Horie of the Bishop Museum Library was also a great help, answering my questions and sending me materials from the library. She compiled the Nakuina biographical material with the help of Leinaala Simmons' and John Charlot's notes and collection of photocopied material, and accompanied me on my visits to Aunty Sarah on a number of occasions. Mahalo nui loa, e Luka. Verlie Ann Malina-Wright, Mahealani McClellan, and Oakleigh Akaka of the Kamehameha Schools Continuing Education Program helped make every step of the translation project move along smoothly, and Kawao Durante gave her support from the start. To Dennis Kawaharada, my friend and editor, he lei nou, no kou lokomaika'i.

Esther T. Mookini
Honolulu, 1992

In Memory of
Sarah Keliʻilolena Lum Nākoa
(September 2, 1911–June 14, 1990)

THE WIND GOURD OF LAʻAMAOMAO

Kūanuʻuanu was Pākaʻa's father and the kahu iwikuamoʻo of Keawenuiaʻumi, who was the aliʻi of the island of Hawaiʻi. The aliʻi was the son of the aliʻi ʻUmi and ʻUmi's wife Kapukini.[1] Kūanuʻuanu was on very good terms with Keawenuiaʻumi, his hānai, but a time came when the kahu felt a growing desire to tour the other islands of this archipelago.

One morning while Kūanuʻuanu was ministering to the personal needs of the aliʻi, he decided the time was right to petition the aliʻi for permission to go on a sightseeing tour: "Ē my haku aliʻi, if you feel love for your kanaka, please allow him to visit the other islands. I'll return quickly. With so many other kahu, you won't be inconvenienced; however, should you find that you are unhappy and need me, and I haven't returned yet, send an ʻelele for me and I'll come back."

When he heard his kahu's request, Keawenuiaʻumi felt heavy-hearted because he didn't want to be without his kahu's expert care. However, since Kūanuʻuanu agreed to return if an ʻelele came to get him, the aliʻi agreed to the request: "Why not? Since you're planning to come right back, I won't detain you. You've been with me a long time and have taken good care of me, and I've always treated you well. Go sightseeing with my blessing. May the akua and ʻaumākua, yours and mine, watch over us until we meet again."

Cheered by his haku's consent, Kūanuʻuanu quickly gathered his kapa, malo, and other belongings for the voyage. He left the aloaliʻi at Waipiʻo, Hawaiʻi, boarded one of the aliʻi's canoes, and set off. He landed at the shady breadfruit trees of Lele in Lahaina, Maui. Since he was a kahu of Keawenuiaʻumi, the aliʻi of Hawaiʻi, and kokoaliʻi, of royal blood, he was well received by all the Maui aliʻi residing at Lahaina. As the kahu iwikuamoʻo of an aliʻi, he knew all the artful activities and amusements of the aloaliʻi and participated with the others in them.

One day when the sea was unruffled by the wind, the famous waves of ʻUo began to break gently. Excited, the kamaʻāina hurried out to surf and Kūanuʻuanu joined them to show that this keiki of Hawaiʻi was a skillful surfer. The ali'i of Maui were impressed by his surfing as he rode swiftly on the waves without getting wet; he wasn't overwhelmed by the surf as he rode the waves breaking to the right, then to the left. His body looked magnificent as he stood up on the surfboard and rode toward shore. When he knelt with his arms outstretched, he looked like a manu ka'upu treading the surface of the sea. His fame as a surfer spread all over Maui.

Kūanu'uanu remained about two months in Lahaina then set off in his canoe and landed at Waikīkī because it was one of the areas where the ali'i of O'ahu had always resided.

At the news of the arrival of the kahu iwikuamo'o of Keawenuia'umi, the ali'i 'aimoku of Hawai'i, these O'ahu ali'i sent an 'elele to bring him to the place where they lived. The O'ahu ali'i welcomed him, and he satisfied their curiosity about Keawenuia'umi and the aloali'i of Hawai'i. Then the O'ahu ali'i ordered the maka'āinana to bring 'ai, i'a, and other nourishments, and Kūanu'uanu feasted until he was satisfied by the generosity of the ali'i and maka'āinana of O'ahu.

After his stay on O'ahu, Kūanu'uanu boarded his canoe again and went to Kaua'i. He toured the island and liked it so much, he settled in Kapa'a. He prospered during his stay, so the men, women, and children of Kapa'a befriended him. It was always like this: people became fast friends with even a malihini if he were prosperous.

Among the crowd of people who came to visit him and make his acquaintance, Kūanu'uanu met an attractive young girl named La'amaomao—the most beautiful girl in Kapa'a. At their first meeting, Kūanu'uanu wanted her for his wife, in accordance with the marriage customs in Hawai'i at that time, and the girl also desired him and consented to be his wife. Twenty days after their first meeting, they were married. Many young boys of Kaua'i desired La'amaomao and wanted to marry her, but she chose this keiki of Hawai'i, and he made her a happy wife. She was a cherished keiki, brought up with care and refinement.[2] Her parents were related to kāhuna, so although they were landless, without moku, kalana, or ahupua'a, they were people of some status.

During his stay on Kaua'i, Kūanu'uanu lived like a maka'āinana, without revealing he was of ali'i blood. Because La'amaomao's parents thought he was just a vagabond, they strongly disapproved of the marriage, and Kūanu'uanu had to be patient during these difficult times with his wife's 'ohana.

Kūanu'uanu planted 'uala, kalo, mai'a, kō, and other useful plants for their livelihood. Two months after they were married, Laʻamaomao felt the discomfort of pregnancy, and the couple was cheered: this keiki would support and care for them in their old age.

Soon after Laʻamaomao discovered her pregnancy, an ʻelele from Keawenuiaʻumi came and found Kūanuʻuanu. After an exchange of greetings, the ʻelele said, "I've been ordered by your haku to bring you back. You must return—he's been patient with the incompetence of his other kahu, but he can't stand it any longer, so he sent me with this appeal to you: 'Tell my kahu I'm helpless without him. I have many other kahu, but they're ill-trained, so I'm greatly inconvenienced. He's been gone too long. Perhaps now he's satisfied with his travels and will return as he promised.'"

When Kūanuʻuanu heard this appeal, love for his hānai welled up in him, and tears filled his eyes. He regretted having left his hānai in untrained hands. He told the ʻelele, "ʻAe, let's return to my aliʻi. I've become a kamaʻāina in this new land and married my wife. Now that she's pregnant, who will care for her and the child? My wife's ʻohana won't give us anything. If I leave, my wife and child will have to beg for food from other people because what we've planted won't be ready for harvest. But I can't be bound here by love for my wife and child. These bones belong to my hānai—he could bake my head in an imu to satisfy his anger if I disobeyed him."[3]

That evening Kūanuʻuanu sat in silence with his wife knowing he would have to leave soon. In a quiet moment he told her he had to return to his hānai, then gave her instructions about their keiki: "I'm returning to Hawaiʻi because my haku, Keawenuiaʻumi, has ordered me to do so through his ʻelele. You'll remain here on Kauaʻi. Should you give birth to a girl give her your family's name. However, should you give birth to a boy, call him Pākaʻa, a name given to my aliʻi for his peeled, cracked, smelly, scaly, chapped skin, which he got from drinking the ʻawa of Panaʻewa.[4]

"I've kept a secret from you: I'm not lōpā. I'm Keawenuiaʻumi's kahu iwikuamoʻo." For the first time Laʻamaomao knew her husband was a high-ranking aliʻi. A few days later, he was ready to depart, so Kūanuʻuanu embraced his wife, shared expressions of love with all the kamaʻāina he had lived with on Kauaʻi, boarded the canoe of the ʻelele, and returned to Hawaiʻi. Upon his return, his haku and close friends greeted him affectionately, and his haku gave back to him his former positions in court and his former ahupua'a.

La'amaomao gave birth to a son, whom she named Pāka'a, according to the instructions of his father. She had hoped the birth of her keiki would reconcile her with her parents, but it didn't—her parents were still angry about her marriage to Kūanu'uanu and called the child a keiki kauwā. Her parents believed their daughter's beauty could have gained her a husband who ruled an ahupua'a, or perhaps a kalana, so he could provide for them in their old age. Instead, La'amaomao had been stubborn and married a vagrant, so even after she became pregnant, her parents felt bitter toward her.

The keiki was sturdy and healthy, but when La'amaomao brought him to the hale of her parents, they cruelly rejected the two of them.[5] She went to live with her keiki on a cape near the cliffs at the beach in Kapa'a, Kaua'i, where she provided for him alone at first.

Among the members of her 'ohana, only her brother felt compassion for La'amaomao. His name was Ma'ilou. His sister was his favorite from the time she was an infant. He was the brother who looked after his sister and raised her, the one who carried her affectionately on his back, hips, and shoulders. After their parents cruelly banished his sister from home, he went to live with her at the beach, helping to provide for and watch over the keiki.

Ma'ilou was a skillful bird-catcher and went into the mountain forest everyday to support the three of them. He was also known for his wit and skill at word-play.

One day he and his sister were desperate for food, so La'amaomao sent Ma'ilou to ask for some from her brothers, her maternal uncles and aunts, and the neighbors of her parents, all of whom had loved the two of them previously and would have given the two anything they wanted; but now they all refused to invite these dear ones into their hale because they didn't want to anger the parents.

La'amaomao and Ma'ilou became partners in bringing up Pāka'a. One day, when Pāka'a was old enough to speak his mind, he asked his mother, "Who is my father?"

She replied, "Ma'ilou is your father."

"You're big, Ma'ilou is small, and I'm tall, even though I'm still very young. Perhaps my father is someone else," said the keiki.[6]

His mother insisted, "'A'ole, Ma'ilou is your father."

Pāka'a continued to pester his mother about the identity of his father. Finally, weary of her keiki's persistent curiosity, she told him the truth: "Kā, how insistent you are! I told you before Ma'ilou is your father. He's provided for you and nurtured you. But he's really my brother. As for your real father, you must look for him. You've never met him. Since you insist on knowing everything, I'll tell you this: to find him, you must look to the east, where the sun rises and a certain local wind blows. Your father lives there."

The keiki was satisfied with this answer, thinking how he knew all along that his father wasn't Ma'ilou, but someone else. He also knew he couldn't find his father now, even if he wanted to, because he didn't have a canoe and he wasn't old enough to travel the seas between the islands; so he quietly restrained his longing to meet his real father. When the time was right, Pāka'a would search for him.

During his childhood, it was already evident that Pāka'a was skillful, intelligent, clever, and hard-working. He wandered here and there and saw men and women working adeptly at different tasks. He sat and watched them carefully, learning the right way to farm, snare birds, carve canoes, fish, and perform other skillful works of the people of old Hawai'i. After observing closely these occupations, he decided to become a fisherman and tried very hard to master all the traditional fishing lore of that time.

During mālolo season, the kānaka went out to sea in their canoes and returned with mālolo.[7] Occasionally, charitable people gave Pāka'a, La'amaomao, and Ma'ilou a few mālolo; but not much, just enough for a single meal.

Pāka'a complained to La'amaomao, "Why is it we don't get to eat mālolo more often? When we're given any, we get only a few while those people in that kauhale eat mālolo all the time."

"Perhaps Ma'ilou, your uncle, doesn't care to go fishing; he enjoys his work of snaring birds and likes to spend his time trudging about without a care in the mountains," responded his mother.

"Why can't I go fishing with the adults—then I could get a share of the catch," said Pāka'a.

His mother replied, "You're inexperienced at fishing and don't know how to swim yet. What if you fell into the ocean and drowned!"

Pāka'a answered, "While you were busy at home, I learned to swim at the beach with the other children, so you don't have to worry about me drowning."

Recently, Pāka'a had seen Ma'ilou at sea in a small racing canoe, so he told his mother, "When Ma'ilou returns, ask him to carry his racing canoe to the water for me. I'll use it as my fishing canoe." "You're a very, very insistent keiki! If that's what you want, go with those mālolo fishermen tomorrow. We'll see what your pile of fish will look like, you quarrelsome keiki!"

After choosing to become a fisherman, Pāka'a had an idea about how to propel his fishing canoe without paddling. He had seen how far out to sea the kānaka had to paddle in search of schools of mālolo, out to where the ocean was deep blue and the mountain ridges of Kaua'i were nearly hidden by the sea.[8] Pāka'a knew it was very tiring to paddle so far out and return home.

After his mother angrily agreed to let him go, Pāka'a prepared his equipment for mālolo fishing. Besides gathering the usual mālolo fishing gear, he cut two straight poles, each an anana and a muku long. He also got rolls of his mother's lau hala and wove a small rectangular mat. Then he secured two corners of the mat to one pole; to the other pole, he secured another corner of the mat. Finally, he lashed the second pole to the middle of the first, creating a mast and sail for his fishing canoe. Using this sail, he wouldn't have to tire out his shoulders paddling.

That evening Ma'ilou returned from the mountains with some birds. He plucked and singed the birds, then broiled them over the fire, and when they were cooked, the three of them ate.

Then La'amaomao spoke: "Ē Ma'ilou, tomorrow morning, before you rush off to the mountains, carry your old canoe to the sea for Pāka'a. Our keiki has been pestering me all day about going mālolo fishing. I refused to give in, but he wouldn't stop. This demanding, persistent keiki is too much. Where does his stubbornness come from? Perhaps he takes after his father." (La'amaomao conveniently forgot how stubborn she had been when she married Kūanu'uanu.)

Ma'ilou agreed with her. "We have birds to eat and are given mālolo. But the mālolo we get from that kauhale isn't enough for the keiki of Kūanu'uanu, so he stubbornly insists on going mālolo fishing himself."

Pāka'a said, "Don't stop me from going. I'm going fishing for the three of us. Perhaps I'll get the entire catch, many kāuna of mālolo, not just leftovers like we had today—scraps, bait fish, and scrapings from the teeth of others."

6

Maʻilou was shamed by the keiki's answer, so he said, "'Ae, you're right, keiki. Go mālolo fishing tomorrow. We won't stop you."

Pākaʻa told him, "Let's go and tighten the lashings of the little canoe to prepare it for sea."

"'Ae," said Maʻilou.

That evening Maʻilou and Pākaʻa prepared the canoe and all the gear necessary for mālolo fishing. The following morning the two woke up early and went down to the canoe, into which Pākaʻa placed his water gourd and the poles and mat.

When Maʻilou saw the keiki's gear, he asked, "What are you going to do with those two poles? And what's that floor mat for?"

"Wait—when you get an answer to one question, then ask another. Two questions can't be answered at the same time. You're like an inquisitive child."

"Your mysterious work is making me inquisitive, ē ke keiki," replied Maʻilou. "Here you're going fishing, and you're preparing two poles and a floor mat to catch your mālolo. The others will roar with laughter at you."

"My dear uncle, you're wrong. This pole is my mast, this other pole is my boom, and this mat is my sail. You know we have to go far out to sea to find a school of mālolo. When it's time to return, I'll set up my mast and sail, and let the gentle wind of Kapaʻa carry me back here to the beach. All I'll have to do is steer with the paddle at the stern of the canoe, so my shoulders won't get tired from paddling. Now do you understand?"

"'Ae, now I understand, my keiki," said Maʻilou. "You'll become famous—the first to use a sail on a fishing canoe to spare the shoulders from paddling."

Then the two of them carried the canoe to the water and prepared it for sea. When it was ready, Pākaʻa jumped in, sat at the stern, seized the paddle, and set off. Pākaʻa already knew how to handle a canoe from watching his uncle and others who knew how to paddle. He paddled gently; the sea was rather calm, and the canoe went foward as well as any canoe with a strong, skillful person paddling at the stern. Pākaʻa joined the fishing-canoe fleet and paddled along with them.

When the kānaka noticed Pākaʻa, they shouted, "Hey! Here comes Laʻamaomao's keiki alone in his canoe."

"Where's his uncle?" someone asked.

"This is the first time the keiki's been allowed to go fishing, and he's all by himself," said another.

Someone else added, "His uncle is doing what he loves best—snaring birds."

That's how the kānaka talked until they got to a place where they thought a school of mālolo might be. As they approached, the head fisherman called out for everyone to prepare the canoes. Some of the canoes were lined up and moved forward together to drive the mālolo into the net set by the other canoes.[9] Pāka'a's canoe was in the middle of the line. The canoes on the outside of the line got to the nets more quickly than the canoes in the middle, so the people in the outside canoes were able to take mālolo from the net before the others did.

When Pāka'a saw this, he said to himself, "Those kānaka in the canoes at the corners of the net are taking fish already. I'll move over there." He stalled his canoe with his paddle, then went around to one of the outside corners of the net and maneuvered quickly in among the canoes that were already there.

The adults tried to block Pāka'a from the net, shouting at him to get back, but he pretended not to hear them. Lifting the edge of the net where the hau floaters were attached, he snatched up the mālolo stuck there and put them into his canoe. Moving to the outside allowed Pāka'a to take many mālolo from the fleet's net before the common catch was hauled in.

When it was time to return, all those who helped with the fishing received their shares from the common catch. Combining his share with what he had grabbed from the net, Pāka'a had two ka'au, or eighty, mālolo.

As the fleet was preparing to return, Pāka'a threw out a challenge: "Say, who dares to race with me? Our mālolo will be the bet. If you beat me, you'll get my fish; if I beat you, I'll get yours."

A large kanaka in a one-man canoe took up the challenge of the small keiki.

"Let's you and me bet," said the kanaka.

"How many mālolo do you have?" asked Pāka'a.

"Two kāuna," answered the kanaka.

Pāka'a replied, "That's not a fair bet because you have only eight fish. If your catch were as big as mine, I'd race with you."

"How many mālolo do you have?" the kanaka asked.

"I have two ka'au."

When the others in the fleet heard how much fish Pāka'a had, they

8

became greedy. Some kānaka called out, "If you want to wager your fish, we'll bet with you. There are eight of us in our canoe, and each of us have ten mālolo, two kāuna plus two extra fish for each—altogether two ka'au, the same number you have."

"It's up to you," said Pāka'a. "If all of you agree to race against me, I'm ready. I think I can beat you. But you see I'm just a small keiki, not old enough to put on a malo while the eight of you in your canoe are adults with yellowed teeth. You may think you don't have to worry about me. No offense, but I won't be last. I'm not afraid to race—otherwise, I wouldn't have challenged you in the first place."

The kānaka answered together, "We accept your challenge, so let's race."

"Agreed, so give me your fish, " said Pāka'a,

"'A'ole," they said. "We should hold all the fish."

"'A'ole," countered Pāka'a. "If I lose, it would be easy for you to come and take the fish from me because I'm just a keiki. But what if I win? You might not want to give up the fish when I come for them, and I'm not strong enough to take them from you. Then I'd have tired out my shoulders with paddling for nothing."

"You're right, ē ke keiki," they said. "So you hold the fish then."

Pāka'a paddled close to the side of the big canoe and the kānaka transferred their fish to his canoe. Then the kānaka said, "The first canoe on dry sand will be the winner. Agreed?"

Pāka'a agreed. When the two canoes were ready, a kanaka in another canoe stood to line up the two canoes evenly. Then he chanted, "Kū kū-'ai-moku! Lā-hai-na! 'O-i-a!"

The large canoe surged forward along with the rest of the canoe fleet while Pāka'a just dillydallyed behind the last canoe. The large canoe was far ahead of him when he turned the bow of his canoe into the wind and raised his mast and sail.

When the kānaka in the canoe fleet looked back and saw Pāka'a wasn't paddling, they began to talk. "The keiki is wasting time—why doesn't he start paddling?" one of them asked.

"Auwē! His canoe is turning into the wind at Kualoa and at Hanamanuea," said another.

"What's that thing he's putting up?" a third asked.

"He's setting up a pole and mat—what for?" asked a fourth.

The others ridiculed him. "You're so slow, ē nā keiki!" they shouted.

"You knew you couldn't outpaddle us, so why did you insist on racing against us?"

With his mast and sail up, Pāka'a turned the bow of his canoe toward land. The wind puffed out the sail, and the canoe began to move swiftly. Pāka'a paddled until the canoe was on course, then just leaned back and steered with his paddle. As his canoe was blown along by the wind, he sang this song:

> The fish of 'Uko'a have vanished,
> The prow whizzes by in the gusty wind,
> Friends are left behind in Puna,
> I'm gone today,
> Out of sight at sea.[10]

Pāka'a looked ahead at the canoe fleet and saw they had gone out ahead very quickly. When the kānaka in the canoe fleet saw something billowing out and coming up fast behind them, they paddled even harder. The other canoes were far in front of Pāka'a, almost out of sight, when Pāka'a first put up his sail, but in no time the keiki was moving along lightly right behind them, almost even with them.

When he sailed by, the kānaka shouted, "Here's the keiki! Here's the keiki with a billowing sail! All he does is sit and steer, while we toil with our paddles!"

Pāka'a's canoe passed by an arm's length from the other canoe. The kānaka were paddling with all their might to keep up with him, but to no avail as Pāka'a sailed past them. When Pāka'a saw the kānaka struggling, he called out loudly:

> Be strong, drink the water of Wailua;
> There is Kalanipuu, the current in the sea.
> He will land,
> The landing of the navigator,
> The ulua of the diver,
> The breath of the kahuna—land;
> Be strong, land the canoe,
> The first-born keiki will be the first to eat
> The first mālolo of Kau.

The kānaka were annoyed by Pāka'a's loud boasting that he would be the first to land and the first to eat the season's mālolo.

But Pāka'a was no longer paying attention to them because he was so far ahead, his canoe carried swiftly along like a dolphin on an ocean swell. In no time he reached shore, so he had two more ka'au of mālolo, and those who had bet with him had nothing.

Meanwhile, the people on shore had seen something billowing coming in from the sea. Not sure what it was, they became excited, crying out repeatedly, "Look at that billowing thing moving over the sea!"

It made straight for the canoe landing, so the people came down to see what it was. As the billowing thing approached, they saw it was a canoe with a mast and a mat sail, and when the canoe was beached, they saw it belonged to Pāka'a, the keiki of La'amaomao.

On the beach he was surrounded by the people, who praised him for his cleverness and intelligence in inventing something new—a sail for a fishing canoe to spare his shoulders from the exhaustion of paddling.

Some of the people helped him carry his canoe onto dry sand, and Pāka'a gave a mālolo to each of them. They were pleased and appreciated the keiki's generosity.

He took down the mast, bundled up the sail, tidied up the canoe, then put the rest of the fish into his lau hala bag, swung it onto his back, and returned to his mother's cave.

Arriving at the mouth of the cave, he didn't see his mother, so he called out, "Are you there?"

"'Ae."

"Here's some fish for us," said Pāka'a.

"How many fish?"

"I have my own two ka'au of mālolo, and I raced against eight kānaka and beat them, so I have their two ka'au as well—one hundred and sixty mālolo in all. I gave some fish away to the people who helped me carry my canoe onto the beach."

"I'll no longer be looked down on, because now I have some fish," his mother said. "Thanks to you we'll eat mālolo. My only hānai, ē ke keiki, you've done well. You bring me life."

When Ma'ilou returned in the evening and saw the great pile of fish, he also praised Pāka'a. That evening they ate the mālolo with great relish until they were full and contented. They didn't eat birds because they were tired of eating birds; besides, the birds had a terrible odor. La'amaomao sent fish to the kauhale whose people had given her fish earlier, telling them the fish she was giving them were caught by her keiki.

11

Many months passed and Pāka'a grew exceedingly tall.

Pa'iea was the ali'i of Kaua'i when Pāka'a was born, an ali'i nui because of his kupuna. Pa'iea decided he wanted to tour all the islands of Hawai'i, so he sent an 'elele for all his kāhuna and kilo to come and determine the right time to travel.

The kāhuna and kilo read the signs and revealed their findings: "Ē ke ali'i, we've observed the signs. Nothing obstructs your path. The way is clear."

Pa'iea was very pleased and began planning his itinerary. On the advice of his kāhuna and kilo, Pa'iea decided to travel around Kaua'i first, then visit the other islands.

The next day, the news of who in the aloali'i would travel with Pa'iea was announced, and rumor of the tour around Kaua'i spread to the back-country.

There, the maka'āinana prepared 'ai, i'a, and everything else proper for a visit from the aloali'i. They heaped up bountiful provisions not only for Pa'iea and his kānaka, but also for the 'ōhua of the ali'i, since it was customary for a travelling ali'i to take along with him a great many 'ōhua as well as some po'e pipili wale.

The news of Pa'iea's tour reached Kapa'a, where Pāka'a and others lived, and some of the people there wanted to join the tour; but only those people closely related to Pa'iea or to the 'ōhua of Pa'iea's aloali'i could go; people with no rights (kuleana) and no blood ties to either the ali'i Pa'iea or to some of his 'ōhua weren't supposed to go; if they did, they would become kauwā—put to work until they were worn out; so it was in the aloali'i.

Such was the practice of hale ho'opili wale in ancient times. If one had rights or connections, one could live as a dependent in the aloali'i.[11]

When Pāka'a saw the crowd of people getting ready to leave their homes and go travelling with Pa'iea, he asked one of them, "Why are you gathering your things together and rolling them up into those 'ope'ope?"

"We want to go sightseeing with Pa'iea, our ali'i. We heard he's planning to tour Kaua'i, then O'ahu and Maui. Perhaps he'll go as far as Hawai'i."

"Where are these places—O'ahu, Maui, and Hawai'i?" asked Pāka'a. "Are they windward of us?"

"We've never seen these islands," they said.

"Let's all go sightseeing with the ali'i," said Pāka'a.

They replied, "That's up to you."

Pāka'a wanted very much to go, so he went home to ask his mother for permission.

His mother didn't give him permission right away. She thought seriously about her keiki's request to join the royal tour, then replied, "Perhaps it's not good for you to go because you might be scolded and treated cruelly and sent to do menial tasks by the 'ōhua of the ali'i."

Pāka'a replied, "Will I be treated cruelly if I pay attention and agree to do these menial tasks? I'll fetch water and do other small tasks appropriate for children. Those tasks appropriate for adults, the adults will do."

Because her keiki's answer was wise and unassuming, La'amaomao agreed to let him go.

Pa'iea's tour of Kaua'i lasted six months.

During this tour, Pāka'a went along not as an 'ōhua of the ali'i, but as a ho'opili wale of an 'ōhua of the ali'i; he was sent on errands and put to hard work not only by the 'ōhua on whom he was dependent, but by another kanaka who was very rude and very loud. No one knew this kanaka was sending Pāka'a on small errands, so when it was time to divide the ali'i's gifts, Pāka'a got nothing. But in spite of this harsh treatment, Pāka'a was patient and persevering. What was important to him was seeing different places and also learning the ways of the aloali'i— how things operated and how things were prepared; he had decided that if Pa'iea went to Hawai'i, he, Pāka'a, would go along, and if his father were still alive, Pāka'a would join the aloali'i there. The training he received on Pa'iea's tour would prepare him for the aloali'i on Hawai'i. Pāka'a hoped to impress Keawenuia'umi with his skills and become someone important to the ali'i.

On his tour of Kaua'i, Pa'iea had more than enough 'ai and i'a to eat, and his 'ōhua were treated with the same generosity as he was. They received so much 'ai they threw some away, scattering it about and wasting it, the 'ai which was the wealth of the maka'āinana of Kaua'i.

Traveling with an ali'i was no hardship for the 'ōhua since it was customary for the maka'āinana to feed the touring court. When an ali'i went traveling, the 'ōhua rejoiced because they knew they would eat well. As the ancients said, "A royal tour is like a lei palaoa, done in grand style, but when you return home, you're on your own."

Pāka'a saw all the famous places of Kaua'i on this tour; when it was over, he returned to Kapa'a and his mother. A few days later, it was announced Pa'iea was going to tour O'ahu and the other islands, so the 'ōhua began getting ready to go.

Pāka'a heard the news and went quickly to talk to his mother about going: "Ē my dear mother, you've brought me up alone in days gone by; now please let me to go with Pa'iea on his tour of O'ahu. Perhaps he might even go as far as Hawai'i, and I might find my father if he's still alive."

"'Ae, go," said his mother. "But go with humility and modesty; be quiet, and listen carefully, and carry out carefully and with patience and perseverance all work assigned to you. Be patient until you get to Hawai'i. Your father should be at the cliffs of Waipi'o. If he's not there, he might be in Hilo. Pay attention to what is said, and when you arrive in the presence of Keawenuia'umi, you'll know you've arrived at the place where your father lives.

"When you reach the aloali'i, look around and you'll see two gray-haired old men—one of them will be your haku and the other, your father. The gray-haired old man with a red feather cloak about his shoulders, a lei palaoa around his neck, and a fan in his hand will be your haku, Keawenuia'umi. The other gray-haired old man holding a kāhili will be your father, Kūanu'uanu. Don't be afraid. Go and sit on your father's lap. He'll look at you and ask your name. Tell him Pāka'a is your name— you were named for Keawenuia'umi's 'awa-wrinkled skin. Then he'll recognize you and say, 'The sky above, the earth below, life, honors, and riches are yours, my keiki.' Then you'll stop taking orders from the shiftless and the worthless because you'll have arrived at the place of your haku and your father. Your father is an ali'i of Hawai'i and the kahu iwikuamo'o of Keawenuia'umi."

Then La'amaomao lifted the lid of a large calabash and took out a small, long, highly polished gourd in a woven bag. The gourd was covered securely. She turned to her keiki and said, "I'm giving you this gourd which belonged to your extraordinary kupunawahine for whom I was named. Her bones are inside the gourd. While she was alive, she controlled all the winds of the islands—she had them under a supernatural power. She gathered all the winds and put them into this gourd, where they're still kept. She memorized one by one the names of all the winds from Hawai'i to Ka'ula. On windless days, she could remove the cover and call out the name of a wind, and the wind in this gourd would blow.

This gourd, called 'the wind gourd of Laʻamaomao,' was famous.

"Before she died, she entrusted me to put her bones inside this gourd and care for them until I had a child. Then I was to give the gourd to the child to watch over. You're my only child, so now I'm giving the gourd to you. You must look after it according to the wishes of your extraordinary kupunawahine.

"You must care for this gourd because it has been handed down from the kupuna. This gourd has great value—you may not think so now, but when you sail with the aliʻi and arrive at an area where no wind blows and the canoes are becalmed, say that the winds are at your command; all you have to do is call, and the winds will blow.

"When you're laughed at, remove the lid of the gourd and call for a wind. The wind will blow and bring the canoes to shore. The aliʻi will be grateful to you, and you'll be loved and valued by him."

Before Pākaʻa sailed off, Laʻamaomao taught him the names of all the winds, along with the prayers, songs and chants concerning them, and when she was done, Pākaʻa had memorized everything. Then he took the wind gourd and tied it with a cord he had made, prepared his other things for the voyage, and left home.

It was said Paʻiea left with a grand traveling company, with many aliʻi and kaukau aliʻi as well as many ʻōhua and kānaka hoʻopili wale and kānaka alualu aliʻi wale.

It was also said that the wind of the sea of Kaʻieʻiewaho was calm when the great number of canoes and people left on this glorious voyage of Paʻiea, the aliʻi of Kauaʻi and the light in the heavens above. He landed first at Waikīkī and was treated with hospitality and honor by all the aliʻi of Oʻahu.

Paʻiea spent several days resting and relaxing on Oʻahu, then continued on to Kaunakakai, Molokaʻi, and from there went east along the southern coast to Pūkoʻo, where he rested again.

Some of the people had joined the tour only to see Oʻahu, so when that part of the trip was over, they returned to Kauaʻi.

The aliʻi rested and enjoyed his stop at Pūkoʻo then sailed until he landed at Malu-ʻUlu-o-Lele at Lahaina, Maui. There he had some pleasant moments surfing the famous waves of ʻUo. Then Paʻiea sailed again and landed at Hāna.

From Hāna, he sailed to Kohala, on Hawaiʻi. The people of Hawaiʻi saw the fleet off Kohala filling the sea of ʻAlenuihāhā and were afraid because they thought the canoes were war canoes. They prepared to defend themselves against an attack.

When Paʻiea landed, however, he was recognized as the aliʻi of Kauaʻi, and the people of Hawaiʻi were relieved and welcomed him with honor. An ʻelele was sent to Waipiʻo to inform Keawenuiaʻumi about Paʻiea's landing, and Keawenuiaʻumi sent several ʻelele back to invite Paʻiea to his aloaliʻi.

After receiving this invitation, Paʻiea sailed with his canoe fleet to Waipiʻo, while some of the people trekked overland. When the fleet landed at Waipiʻo, where Keawenuiaʻumi had remained with his guards, the two aliʻi met and greeted each other with warm affection.

At this initial meeting, there was a great feeling of love and joy between the two aliʻi, and between the aliʻi and the makaʻāinana. The makaʻāinana of Waipiʻo and neighboring areas brought generous amounts of food for the people of Kauaʻi, who ate until they were nauseated and couldn't eat any more. They boasted, "We ate the bounty of Hawaiʻi, brought by request, and we stuffed ourselves until the food backed up our throats." It was said that on the first day of Paʻiea's arrival, the sun was hidden and the land darkened by the smoke from imu in which puaʻa, ʻīlio, moa, pelehū, kalo, ʻuala, and all kinds of other food were being cooked.

So it went until the bountiful food was all consumed or wasted. Then the flow of food began to diminish, except for some provisions to the aloaliʻi of Paʻiea. When the back-country yielded no more food, the poʻe hoʻopili wale and the ʻōhua of Paʻiea were in trouble. The great number of ʻōhua who had accompanied the aliʻi were very hungry. Some of them wandered off to the kauhale of the kamaʻāina and made friends with them, but the majority remained without provisions.

This is the way it was from long ago—at first, the malihini and the kamaʻāina enjoyed themselves, but in the end, the malihini were nothing special and had to look after their own needs.

After arriving at the aloaliʻi of Keawenuiaʻumi, Pākaʻa looked around for his father. When he saw a gray-haired old man holding a kāhili, he remembered the words of his mother and decided it was his good fortune to have found his father.

When the starvation and hunger of Pākaʻa mā, and the ʻōhua of the aliʻi waxed great, the ʻaipuʻupuʻu of Paʻiea began to worry that their aliʻi would have to go without ʻai and iʻa.

As for Pākaʻa, he had been sent on errands by this lōpā or that lōpā ever since coming to Hawaiʻi, but now all of these poʻe hoʻopili wale went hungry because there was no food for them.

The kamaʻāina had food, so Keawenuiaʻumi and his ʻōhua had an ample supply, but Pākaʻa and the ʻōhua of Paʻiea could only close their eyes and swallow their saliva when they saw the others eat.

One day, after Pākaʻa had discovered his father, and the crowd from Kauaʻi was still miserable from hunger, Pākaʻa told them confidently, "I'll get some food for us if I can reach those gray-haired old men sitting there."

One kanaka retorted, "That's an empty boast! You can't get anything from them."

Pākaʻa replied, "I may not be able to reach those old men who are starving us, but if I can, I'll get ʻai and iʻa for us and we'll survive."

The kānaka answered sarcastically, "You think you're privileged? You'll get kicked in the balls!"

"What makes you think you'll get something, little boy, while Paʻiea gets nothing. What a fool!"

"Are you looking for a fight? Can't you see that those two old men are guarded on all sides by koa and ilāmuku? If you think you can just walk up to those two, you're wrong. Those koa will kill you for breaking the kapu."

Thus the kānaka ridiculed the keiki for claiming he could get some food from Keawenuiaʻumi and Kūanuʻuanu. But Pākaʻa was patient as usual with all their vicious remarks and responded without rudeness.

"I'm not frightened by your fearful talk. I face death with the hope of life. Nothing will be gained by staying here and starving to death. This body may be injured or even killed in the presence of those gray-haired old men. But there's a chance all of you might survive and most of you might return to Kauaʻi, our home, not starve to death here. So it's better for me to die trying to reach those two old men than for all of us to do nothing and die from starvation here."

Then Pākaʻa opened the little kapa bundle which his mother had given him, and for the first time on this trip, he put on some of his clothes—a white malo and a fine, gauzy kapa kīhei; he also carried a fan. When he was dressed, he went forward without timidity or fear.

In the aloaliʻi, the aliʻi was set apart from the ilāmuku and the koa, and

17

the makaʻāinana were kept even farther away. The area designated for the aliʻi was kapu—no one could enter there, only his kahu iwikuamoʻo. If someone without the right approached the aliʻi, that person would be put to death.

Pākaʻa approached the assembly guarding the aliʻi, then stopped and waited for a chance to go forward. When he saw a small opening where the koa stood, he moved there quickly. He kept an eye on the koa and ilāmuku and saw they were relaxed and inattentive, so he wasn't recognized as an intruder. He tiptoed quietly past the kapu sticks marking the aliʻi's kapu area. As he moved toward the place where Keawenuiaʻumi and Kūanuʻuanu sat, he was spotted for the first time by the koa and ilāmuku. They began shouting, "That keiki is trespassing upon the kapu grounds of the aliʻi!" They chased Pākaʻa, grabbed him, and beat him.

Pākaʻa escaped and raced as fast as he could to Kūanuʻuanu. The keiki seized and pulled away the kāhili that Kūanuʻuanu held firmly, then sat on his father's lap.

Kūanuʻuanu was angry and annoyed at the keiki's brazen behavior, so when Pākaʻa sat on his lap, the old man spread his legs apart to make Pākaʻa fall to the ground. But the keiki was quicker than his father—when his father spread his legs, Pākaʻa threw his right leg over his father's right leg, straddling it.

In Hawaiʻi's unwritten laws, only a keiki ponoʻī can sit on his father's lap, so when this keiki sat on Kūanuʻuanu's lap, the old man immediately remembered Laʻamaomao and thought perhaps this was his keiki by her.

Kūanuʻuanu asked, "Whose child are you?"

"Kūanuʻuanu and Laʻamaomao's."

"Are you Pākaʻa?"

"ʻAe, I'm Pākaʻa."

"For whom were you named?"

"For Keawenuiaʻumi."

"So you are the keiki of my journey to Kauaʻi?" Then he embraced the keiki tightly, kissing him and weeping loudly. When the aliʻi heard Kūanuʻuanu's loud weeping, he asked, "Whose keiki is this?"[12]

Kūanuʻuanu answered, "This is my keiki. When I went to visit Kapaʻa, Kauaʻi, I married and my wife became pregnant. Then your ʻelele came and ordered me to return, so I did, leaving my wife with this keiki. I gave him the name of Pākaʻa for you—for the cracked, scaly quality of your skin from ʻawa-drinking."

Keawenuiaʻumi said, "ʻAe, your journey was truly fortunate, for now I have a new kahu. Teach him all you know so he'll be able to perform your duties well. Don't keep anything from him. Make sure he's well trained because you are growing old. You and I don't know how much longer we're going to live. Should you die before me, I'll be helpless without someone to take your place."

"'Ae," Kūanu'uanu responded, "your wishes will be carried out, ē ke ali'i."

Soon after, Keawenuia'umi sent some 'elele to collect goods from the people, and give them as gifts to honor Pāka'a, the keiki of Kūanu'uanu, who would be one of his new kahu. The news of Pāka'a's new status quickly spread to Pa'iea and among all the people of Kaua'i who accompanied him to Hawai'i, including those who had treated Pāka'a badly by ordering him to work like a kauwā or by slandering and ridiculing him.

Hearing the news, the 'ōhua and the kānaka of Pa'iea feared they would be killed for treating Pāka'a badly or depriving him of food. They sighed and groaned, burdened by fear and regret.

However, they were mistaken. Pāka'a wasn't vengeful; rather, he was by nature patient and understanding. When gifts of food were brought to him, he didn't hurry off to eat alone; instead, he gave most of the food to Pa'iea mā and the people of Kaua'i. Pāka'a never forgot to give a share to even the lowliest person. He gave according to each person's rank—if a person was of high rank, the portion was large; if a person was of low rank, the portion was small.

Because of Pāka'a, there was a second feast, a second cooking of pua'a, a second offering of gifts during Pa'iea's sightseeing journey. The first gift-giving ceremony was for Pa'iea; the second was for Pāka'a.

When it became known Pāka'a was the true son of Kūanu'uanu, the personal kahu of Keawenuia'umi, the news spread all over the island of Hawai'i. It was joyful news for the maka'āinana, who had great affection for their haku and were obedient to their ali'i, not denying him anything and agreeable in matters concerning the maka'āinana.

As Pāka'a grew up and got bigger, he became even more handsome and knowledgeable; he became skillful and expert in everything he did in the aloali'i of Keawenuia'umi. He learned the laws of the skies and the nature of the earth; farming and all the activities related to it; astronomy and sailing the seas; navigation and steering a canoe; living in the uplands; and fishing and all the activities related to it. Because Pāka'a was so knowledgeable and skillful, Keawenuia'umi gave him a high position in the aloali'i just under his father, Kūanu'uanu.

Along with Pāka'a's appointment to a high and honored position, Keawenuia'umi also gave him lands, and in turn Pāka'a gave lands to some people of Kaua'i. Recognizing his generosity and compassion, a great many of the people of Kaua'i attached themselves to Pāka'a and remained as his kānaka.

Pa'iea stayed on Hawai'i a long time and became an important and honored person in the aloali'i of Keawenuia'umi and indeed in all of Hawai'i. Pa'iea ate and drank from Pāka'a's bounty. He saw how some of the people of Kaua'i attached themselves to Pāka'a and became his kānaka, including those who had treated the keiki with contempt previously; more than half of those who had come eventually stayed permanently on the island of Hawai'i serving under Pāka'a.

With the help of Keawenuia'umi and Pāka'a, Pa'iea finally returned to Kaua'i honored and laden with goods.

When the ali'i and maka'āinana of Kaua'i saw their ali'i returning home, they felt great love, and wept affectionately for the people who returned with the ali'i and for the people who remained permanently on Hawai'i.

Pa'iea brought with him the gifts which Pāka'a had sent to his mother, La'amaomao, and thereafter, Pāka'a continued to send gifts to his mother.

Pa'iea spread the news of the honors and wealth given to Pāka'a, the keiki of La'amaomao, who had become an important person in the aloali'i of Keawenuia'umi and also a possessor of lands on Hawai'i.

The people on Kaua'i at first didn't believe the news, but when Pa'iea's fleet brought the gifts Pāka'a had sent to La'amaomao, the ali'i and maka'āinana of Kaua'i were convinced, and La'amaomao became sought after among the people of Kapa'a. The people had behaved in this way since ancient times: if you were poor, you had no friends or companions—not even blood relatives acknowledged you. They would be ashamed if it were known you were related to them. However, if they heard you had become wealthy, you would have blood relatives coming from distant places to visit you. A whole procession of people would make claims on you—blood relatives, acquaintances, and friends. Even hangers-on not related to you would break away from their families and cling to you. One could claim to be a blood relative even though the relationship was only through some family friend. People claimed relationships by saying such things as "This is your sister. A friend of your mother's was a friend of her mother"; or "This is your younger sibling. Your great-great-grandfather lived with his people." People sought relationships in many ways, and sometimes they were very clever in claiming new relatives; and if you listened to these claims, they might sound like the truth. But here's the truth: before you were rich, no one came near you.

When Pāka'a was twenty-five years old, Kūanu'uanu became gravely ill. The medical experts who saw him knew he wouldn't recover because the disease was kohepopo. (This illness is called akepau, or consumption, today.) Kūanu'uanu realized he was dying, so he called Pāka'a and told him, "My days are almost over, so here are my last words to you: Take good care of the ali'i, as you've seen me do. Listen to the ali'i's small talk as well as his important words. Look after the 'ai and i'a of the ali'i, and if they get moldy or rank and he doesn't ask for them right away, place them in the sun to dry, then put them into a gourd for storage; serve him with the fresh fish, the live fish, the growing 'awa and the dried 'awa. Look after the kānaka iki and the kānaka nui, the kānaka ki'eki'e and the kānaka ha'aha'a. My lands are now yours. Look to your haku."[13]

As Kūanu'uanu gave these instructions to Pāka'a in the aloali'i, Keawenuia'umi and his kānaka listened silently.

When Kūanu'uanu died, the sad news spread throughout Hawai'i, and the maka'āinana and ali'i wept mournfully because they felt great love for him. He was congenial and compassionate and understood both the kānaka nui and the kānaka iki. He never neglected or mistreated any of the ali'i who came to the aloali'i of Keawenuia'umi. Because Kūanu'uanu performed so many good deeds, he was greatly loved.

Keawenuia'umi was filled with grief and love for his kahu and mourned over him for many days. When his sadness over the death of his kahu ended, he appointed Pāka'a as his kahu.

Because of his love for Kūanu'uanu, Keawenuia'umi made Pāka'a not only his kahu, but his Lunanui, Pu'ukū, Kilo, and Kuhikuhipu'uone.

Kahikuokamoku was Keawenuia'umi's Kuhinanui and also an aikāne punahele.

Five of the six ali'i who ruled moku on the island of Hawai'i were sons of Keawenuia'umi, who had appointed them to their positions: Mākaha of Ka'ū; Hua'ā of Puna; Kulukulu'ā of Hilo; Wanu'a of Hāmākua; and Wahilani of Kohala. 'Ehu, the ali'i of Kona, was an

21

adopted son of Keawenuia'umi.

Order and justice prevailed in all things under the careful administration of Pāka'a and the island of Hawai'i was at peace. Pāka'a recognized the kānaka iki and the kānaka nui, the kānaka ki'eki'e and the kānaka ha'aha'a, and everyone felt lovingly attached to him.

Keawenuia'umi also loved Pāka'a because Pāka'a was even more skillful than Kūanu'uanu in attending to the ali'i's needs.

However, during this time of happiness in the aloali'i, there were people who envied Pāka'a's honored position and became his enemies. The most evil of his enemies were Ho'okele-i-Hilo and Ho'okele-i-Puna,[14] two experts in sailing canoes. They understood all the lore of their profession, the signs of the heavens and earth, and the calm and stormy days. They knew as much as Pāka'a about sailing, but Pāka'a had one power they didn't have: he could bring forth the winds of Hawai'i from the wind gourd of La'amaomao.

These two kānaka coveted Pāka'a's positions and honors for themselves, so they approached Keawenuia'umi and made small talk, pretending to be wise while acting as tattle-tales and spreading slander in order to turn the ali'i against Pāka'a. They boasted of their knowledge in steering canoes and their good work in the aloali'i. Because of their lies and dishonesty concerning Pāka'a, Keawenuia'umi turned against Pāka'a, and these two leaders gained control over the ali'i through their deceit.

Thereafter, the ali'i began to treat his virtuous kauwā with contempt, and it became evident that Pāka'a was no longer the ali'i's favorite.

Pāka'a wasn't aware he had lost favor with the ali'i until the ali'i took back almost all the lands he had granted Pāka'a earlier, leaving him with only several bits of land in the district of Hilo; and the ali'i took away all the things Pāka'a had been given charge of and put them under the care of Ho'okele-i-Hilo and Ho'okele-i-Puna. Only then did Pāka'a realize he had become nothing to his haku and the ali'i's faith and trust were with his new favorites.

The ali'i didn't stop there in taking things back from Pāka'a. Keawenuia'umi no longer provided for Pāka'a, and the ali'i gave Ho'okele-i-Hilo and Ho'okele-i-Puna the position of ho'okele-wa'a, so the only duties left to Pāka'a were those of Pu'ukū and the job of laying the foundations for hale. If the ali'i went to Hilo or other places around the island and received gifts from the district ali'i and maka'āinana, the two ho'okele-wa'a would see the gifts first and take what they wanted.

Whatever was left over was given to Pāka'a, who would then distribute these leftovers to the other ali'i and the 'ōhua of the ali'i.

The ali'i had taken away so much from him, Pāka'a complained bitterly; not only had he been stripped of his wealth and honors, but also the two kānaka had usurped from him the duties of the ho'okele and the care of the ali'i's canoes.

Since Keawenuia'umi treated Pāka'a with contempt, the other ali'i and the maka'āinana treated him with contempt as well. Now everyone supported Ho'okele-i-Hilo and Ho'okele-i-Puna, who had won promotions and had become the ali'i's favorites.

These kānaka found fault with Pāka'a every day and slandered him in order to drive him from the aloali'i of Keawenuia'umi.

Pāka'a realized his haku no longer wanted him around; anguished and depressed, he decided to leave. He didn't want to take orders from the two kānaka who had been placed above him.

Pāka'a departed deeply hurt and resentful. He didn't return all of the ali'i's personal effects; he packed some of Keawenuia'umi's kapa, malo, and some 'awa and 'awa-drinking utensils inside the wind gourd of La'amaomao. He also took a large paddle called Lapakahoe, named after his younger brother.

Then one night just before midnight Pāka'a left Waipi'o and the glorious court of Keawenuia'umi, the ali'i 'aimoku of Hawai'i.

It was said that the canoe Pāka'a left in was concealed by mats. Bundles of mats had been piled up at the sides and under the canoe until a mound was created, then the real canoe was placed inside of the mat canoe. Thus did Pāka'a escape being killed by Ho'okele-i-Hilo mā.

Ho'okele-i-Hilo mā spied on Pāka'a, and when they found out that Pāka'a had concealed a canoe with matting, they knew he was planning to leave. They watched vigilantly for his departure and as Pāka'a was leaving, they pursued him quickly in order to drown him by swamping and overturning his canoe. Pāka'a wasn't worried, however, because his canoe was swift and the hull was covered, so seawater couldn't get into it; thus, he escaped.

When Pāka'a's canoe was out in the open ocean off Waipi'o, the local winds A'eloa and Holopo'opo'o blew gently and pleasantly, and Pāka'a paddled smoothly along in his small canoe. While it was still daylight, Pāka'a, with his two enemies following behind him, was outside Hilo-pali-kū and at nightfall he approached Hilo.

Hoʻokele-i-Hilo mā chased Pākaʻa until it was dark and Pākaʻa's canoe vanished from sight. Hoʻokele-i-Hilo mā grew tired of the chase and gave up; they returned to Waipiʻo, hoping Pākaʻa had left for good and would never return.

Pākaʻa went on and landed at Hilo where his younger brother Lapakahoe ruled over several ahupuaʻa belonging to Pākaʻa—the lands not taken back by Keawenuiaʻumi.

When Pākaʻa arrived at his younger brother's place, they greeted each other warmly and ate. Then Pākaʻa told him, "Our haku no longer wants me around. He's taken back all the wealth he's given me except for these lands. The time will come when these lands will be snatched from me, too. So here's what I want you to do: remain with our haku while I depart. I don't know where I'm going to live. If our haku takes back this land, remain as a kanaka under him."

Then Pākaʻa took his gourd and paddle, said a warm farewell to his younger brother, and left in his canoe. Pākaʻa paddled over the high seas for a day and a night until he landed on the southern coast of Molokaʻi, below Hoʻolehua.

When Pākaʻa landed on Molokaʻi as a malihini, many kamaʻāina welcomed him warmly.

Hikauhi was one of the beautiful women of the coastal area where Pākaʻa landed; she was the daughter of Hoʻolehua and his wife ʻĪloli, who were the aliʻi of the island. Kaumanamana was another keiki of these two aliʻi and a brother of Hikauhi.

Earlier, Hoʻolehua and ʻĪloli had given Hikauhi as a wife to Pālāʻau, a keiki makua of the area, but when Pākaʻa arrived, Hikauhi no longer thought about Pālāʻau and instead greatly desired Pākaʻa.[15]

Hikauhi's behavior was considered inexplicable, so Hoʻolehua went to talk things out with the parents of Pālāʻau. Pālāʻau agreed to let Hikauhi be Pākaʻa's wife. Because of Pālāʻau's good will, they all lived together as friends, without disagreements.

After Pākaʻa married Hikauhi, they lived together as husband and wife; Pākaʻa had to work hard farming and fishing in this hot, dry place, but since he was an expert in these activities, the couple prospered and lived very comfortably.

Soon Hikauhi became pregnant and gave birth to a son, whom Pākaʻa named Kūapākaʻa. The first part of the name "Kūa" was from the name of Pākaʻa's father, Kūanuʻuanu. To "Kūa," Pākaʻa added "Pākaʻa," referring to the 'awa-wrinkled skin of his haku, Keawenuia'umi, because Pāka'a didn't want this name to be forgotten. Kūapāka'a was raised as a favorite, and as soon as he was able to talk, Pāka'a began to teach the keiki the duties of a kahu and the chants of Keawenuia'umi. He told the keiki, "Let's learn the tasks of our haku, so you'll know them. Then perhaps when the love he once felt for me wells up in his heart again and he searches us out, you'll be prepared to serve him."

Before long, the keiki had learned thoroughly everything his father wished to teach him. Then Pāka'a instructed his keiki in the names of all the winds of each island, and as in other things his father had taught him, the keiki quickly mastered all the knowledge.

When Ho'okele-i-Hilo and Ho'okele-i-Puna first took over, they had the reputation of being prompt in their duties, and skillful and careful in carrying them out, but this was only because Pāka'a was there to look after his ali'i's needs. Pāka'a did those things Ho'okele-i-Hilo mā didn't know how to do, thus insuring his haku would be well cared for. However, Ho'okele-i-Hilo mā had repeatedly abused and complained about Pāka'a, so he left the aloali'i and his haku.

For the first few months after Pāka'a's departure, Keawenuia'umi didn't miss Pāka'a because Ho'okele-i-Hilo mā continued to malign the former kahu, but eventually the ali'i began to notice his new favorites were neglecting his needs. Ho'okele-i-Hilo mā began to exalt themselves, and after awhile disregarded the ali'i's wishes. Everything given to Keawenuia'umi was taken by the two for themselves and their followers, and only the leftovers were passed on to the ali'i. If Keawenuia'umi complained about the small amount he received, the two would lie and say only a small amount was given.

In public, Keawenuia'umi was very patient with their dishonesty, but in private, he shed many tears, blaming himself for being so gullible and for ridiculing Pāka'a, his virtuous and capable kahu, who had taken such good care of him. He confessed to himself, "I was wrong to neglect my kanaka. Now I realize he was treated unfairly."

The more the ali'i was neglected and mistreated, the more he began to miss Pāka'a. He could no longer repress his feelings, and his thoughts wandered here and there as he yearned to hear and see Pāka'a.

Keawenuia'umi's love for Pāka'a grew stronger as the evil deeds of his new favorites grew more frequent, and he began to despise these worthless hoʻokele-waʻa and made up his mind to go and find Pākaʻa.

Keawenuiaʻumi sent an ʻelele to bring kilo, kāhuna, and kuhikuhipuʻuone to advise him as to whether it was right or wrong to search for Pākaʻa. The kilo and kāhuna came and set up a flat surface for divination, while the kilo and kuhikuhipuʻuone looked for signs in the sky and the clouds. When the divinations and observations were over, they told the aliʻi, "The ʻaumākua and the signs in the clouds and sky reveal that if you search for Pākaʻa, you may find him because Pākaʻa is alive. However, there are no directions for finding him; the place where he can be found is hidden from us.

"Don't go looking for him right away, however. First, order all the aliʻi and makaʻāinana to go to the mountain forests to cut down koa trees and make some good canoes for you. Then go in search of your beloved kahu ponoʻī."

After the kāhuna, kilo, and kuhikuhipuʻuone had observed the signs, the aliʻi, makaʻāinana, and kāhuna kālai-waʻa were ordered to go up into the mountains to cut down trees for the canoes the aliʻi wanted. Those who weren't able to go remained behind to farm and cook for those who went.

Keawenuiaʻumi didn't think it would take long to fell the trees for the canoes, but in the end, he was exhausted. Still, "the pelting rains wear down the rock at Kekaʻa."[16]

When the aliʻi and makaʻāinana found a place where tall, straight koa trees suitable for canoes grew, they selected one and began chopping it down. But at the thumping of the kāhuna kālai-waʻa's adzes at the base of the tree, two birds up in the tree began chirping. The kāhuna remarked, "The birds are telling us this tree is rotten."[17]

They examined the tree and found it was indeed rotten, so they chose another tree and began chopping it down. When the tree fell, the two birds cried out again from above, and the kāhuna kālai-waʻa remarked again, "This tree is also rotten—the birds chirped again."

When they examined it, the tree was indeed rotten. Thus, Keawenuiaʻumi and his kānaka worked till exhaustion without accomplishing anything. The archers of the aliʻi shot arrows at the birds; the men with slings flung stones at them; the bird trappers tried to ensnare the birds; the bird catchers tried to capture the birds with birdlime; yet the two birds escaped unharmed—until Pikoiakaʻalalā arrived.

The birds were Pākaʻa's ʻaumākua. They were testing the aliʻi to see

kō and six patches of ʻuala for the six district aliʻi.[20] After the crops were planted, Pākaʻa said to the keiki, "Let's go mauka again for loulu fronds." "'Ae," said the keiki. The two gathered the fronds and made a pile of them beside their hale until Pākaʻa said, "That's enough."

The bird ʻaumākua of Pākaʻa had delayed the cutting of the trees for Keawenuiaʻumi's canoes, so that Pākaʻa could build all the hale, plant the fields of ʻuala and kō, and collect the loulu fronds. The birds had sacrificed themselves for Pākaʻa and Kūapākaʻa. When everything was ready, Pākaʻa waited patiently for his haku's arrival.

The news spread from island to island that Keawenuiaʻumi was planning to search for his kahu Pākaʻa. The people on each island were asked, "Where is this kanaka Pākaʻa?" No one knew the answer.

One night as Keawenuiaʻumi was resting, his spirit met Pākaʻa's spirit, and the aliʻi's spirit said, "I'm searching for you."

Pākaʻa's spirit replied, "If you're searching for me, you'll find me living on Kaʻula."

Keawenuiaʻumi woke up suddenly. He knew it was only a dream, but he felt relieved because Pākaʻa's spirit had revealed to him Pākaʻa's whereabouts.

In the morning the aliʻi sent an ʻelele for his kāhuna, kilo, kuhikuhipuʻuone, and hoʻokele-waʻa, and when they arrived, the aliʻi told them about his dream. They thought carefully about the dream and said, "The akua are hiding Pākaʻa's whereabouts. Pākaʻa is not on Kaʻula."

"The canoes are ready," said the aliʻi. "When shall we depart?"

"We've observed the signs," said the kāhuna. "They indicate your search party should depart during the days of Kū."[21]

The next night, because the aliʻi had been thinking all day about searching for Pākaʻa, his spirit again met Pākaʻa's spirit in a dream. The aliʻi's spirit said, "I'm ready to search for you."

Pākaʻa's spirit answered, "If you come searching for me, you'll find me on Kaʻula."

The aliʻi's spirit said, "During the days of Kū we'll sail in search of you."

The aliʻi woke up with a start and knew he had been dreaming.

When the days of Kū came, the canoes were ready and the search for Pākaʻa began.

Because the kāhuna had told the aliʻi Pākaʻa wasn't on Kaʻula,

29

Keawenuia'umi doubted his dream and decided to land on every island until he got to Ka'ula.

At dawn the canoes left Waipi'o, the ali'i and his kānaka going very orderly, by rank: first, ten one-man canoes; then ten two-man canoes; then ten three-man canoes; then came the majority of kānaka on various kinds of canoes; then the double-hulled canoes of the 'āipu'upu'u, the canoe of the pū-kaua, the canoe of the wāhine, and the canoe of the koa moved ahead; then the canoes of the district ali'i set out—Wahilani of Kohala in front, followed by Wanu'a of Hāmākua; then Kulukulu'ā of Hilo; then Hua'ā of Puna; then Mākaha of Ka'ū; then 'Ehu of Kona. Keawenuia'umi and Kahikuokamoku, the Kuhina Nui, followed in a beautiful double-hulled canoe with a platform built between the two hulls.

The canoes made their first landfall at Lahaina, where the people of Maui were asked about Pāka'a. They reported that he wasn't there. The ali'i spent the night on Maui, then left Lahaina before dawn, still during the days of Kū.

On Moloka'i Pāka'a awakened Kūapāka'a.

"Here you are, still asleep!"

"What is it?"

"Let's go down to the beach. If we don't keep watch, your haku will sail past without our meeting him."

"That's true."

The two got up, gathered their supplies for catching uhu, and took along with them the wind gourd of La'amaomao. They went down to their fishing canoe, climbed in, and paddled out.

Pāka'a held the net and the decoy uhu on a line at the bow of the canoe. There, he wouldn't be recognized by Keawenui-a'umi because a kanaka fishing for uhu always keeps his head down to watch for fish entering his net.[22]

Their wind gourd of La'amaomao was near the stern outrigger boom, and Kūapāka'a was farther back with his father's big paddle, Lapakahoe. As soon as they lowered their stone anchor at the fishing grounds, the first canoes of Keawenuia'umi's fleet arrived—ten one-man canoes, ten two-man canoes, ten three-man canoes. When the double-hulled canoes of the ali'i came into view, Pāka'a and Kūapāka'a saw a fire blazing offshore near Kaunakakai.[23]

"Ē! That's a big fire burning there," said Kūapāka'a. "Perhaps my haku is coming here on that canoe."

Pāka'a said, "No."

"Who, then?"

"Wahilani; Kohala is his."

"Is he an ali'i?"

"He's not an ali'i," said Pāka'a.

Then Wahilani's canoe passed by, and Kūapāka'a called out loudly: "Wahilani, our ali'i of Kohala, goes by. He's not an ali'i, only a kaukauali'i[24] who hides himself in the stands of Kohala cane. The only i'a in his land is the grasshopper—there on the sugarcane leaf, there on the flower-stem of grass.[25] Kohala is a land without any i'a and the only 'ai is the sweet potato. The defect in the land is that Wahilani is not an ali'i, yet he enjoys the bounty of Kohala, so he's called an ali'i."

An ilāmuku of Wahilani asked, "Who is this kanaka shouting at the ali'i?"

"Who indeed?" said Kūapāka'a. "He can't be seen—it's still dark."

Wahilani was peeved that the keiki had said Wahilani wasn't an ali'i and that this was a defect in his land, so he asked, "Where did you hear these things you're recounting, you lying little keiki?"

Angry, he urged his hoewa'a to paddle faster, and they continued on.

After Wahilani passed by, another fire blazed, and Kūapāka'a said to his father, "Ē! There's another fire. Perhaps my haku is on this canoe?"

"No."

"Who, then?"

"Wanu'a; Hāmākua is his."

"Is he an ali'i?"

"He's not an ali'i."

As Wanu'a's canoe passed by, Kūapāka'a called out loudly: "Wanu'a goes by, our ali'i of Hāmākua, yet he's not an ali'i, but a kaukauali'i who traps the puhi of Hāmākua with his fingers. He lays his fingers on the smooth rock with bait and when the small puhi crawl up in the spaces between his fingers he grabs them and tosses them into a gourd.[26] This is how he catches the fish of his land, and this is how he enjoys the bounty of Hāmākua. It's said he's an ali'i, but he's not an ali'i."

"Who is this kanaka shouting at the ali'i?" asked an ilāmuku of Wanu'a.

"Who, indeed?" said Kūapāka'a. "He can't be seen in the darkness." The ali'i was angry as he continued on.

Another fire blazed, and Kūapāka'a asked again, "Is this perhaps my haku?"

"It's not your haku. It's Kulukulu'ā; Hilo is his.

"Is he an ali'i?"

"He's not an ali'i," said Pāka'a.

Then the canoe of Kulukulu'ā passed by, and Kūapāka'a called out in loudly: "Kulukulu'ā goes by, our ali'i of Hilo. He's not an ali'i but merely a kaukauali'i, a catcher of the 'ōpae of Waiākea. After catching the 'ōpae, he puts his coconut fiber snare behind his ear.[27] Since he enjoys the bounty of Hilo, he's called an ali'i."

"Who is this shouting at the ali'i?" asked an ilāmuku of Kulukulu'ā.

"Who, indeed?" Kūapāka'a said. "He can't be seen in the darkness." The ali'i was angry as he continued on.

Another fire blazed, and the keiki asked Pāka'a again, "Is this perhaps my haku?"

"It's not your haku. That's Hua'ā; Puna is his.

"Is he an ali'i?" the keiki asked again.

"He's not an ali'i," replied Pāka'a.

Then the canoe of Hua'ā passed by, and Kūapāka'a called out loudly: "Hua'ā goes by, our ali'i of Puna. He's not an ali'i, but a kaukauali'i, the thorny eyes of the lau hala of Puna.[28] Since he enjoys the bounty of Puna, he's called an ali'i."

An ilāmuku of Hua'ā asked, "Who is this shouting at the ali'i?"

Kūapāka'a said, "Who, indeed? He can't be seen in the darkness." The ali'i was peeved as he continued on.

Another fire blazed, and the keiki asked Pāka'a again, "Is this perhaps my haku?"

"It's not your haku. That's Mākaha; Ka'ū is his."

"Is he an ali'i?" asked Kūapāka'a.

"He's not," said Pāka'a.

Then Mākaha's canoe passed by, and Kūapāka'a called out loudly: "Mākaha goes by, our ali'i of Ka'ū. He's not an ali'i but a kaukauali'i, a dirty-faced one of Ka'ū. He beats the dirt off his body with the 'ilima leaves of the uplands of Kamā'oa. Thus, he takes a bath in his dry, dusty land. All the dirt of the place is gone, except for the dirt behind his ears. Since he enjoys the bounty of Ka'ū, he's called an ali'i."[29]

The ilāmuku of Mākaha asked, "Who is this kanaka shouting at the ali'i?"

"Who, indeed?" said Kūapākaʻa. "He can't be seen in the darkness." The aliʻi was angry as he continued on.

Another fire blazed, and the keiki again asked Pākaʻa, "Perhaps this is my haku?"

"It's not your haku. That's ʻEhu; Kona is his."

"Is he perhaps an aliʻi?" asked Kūapākaʻa.

"He's not an aliʻi, but an ʻuala farmer from the uplands of Nāpuʻu."

Then ʻEhu's canoe passed by, and Pākaʻa called out loudly: "ʻEhu goes by, our aliʻi of Kona. He's not an aliʻi, he's an ʻuala farmer from the uplands of Nāpuʻu. When we were living with Keawenuiaʻumi in Kīholo, ʻEhu came down from the uplands with baskets of ʻuala, and the aliʻi ate until he was full. Ē ʻEhu, because you had so much ʻuala, the aliʻi survived there, and he felt so embarrassed about eating so much, he adopted you as a son. You were given Kona, so now you're called an aliʻi."

An ilāmuku of ʻEhu asked, "Who is this kanaka shouting at the aliʻi?"

"Who indeed," said Kūapākaʻa. "He can't be seen in the darkness."

As the sky brightened, the keiki asked his father, "When will my haku arrive?"

"When you see the first rays of the sun, you'll see your haku. You won't miss him. You'll see his sail doubled down at the middle to show Kāʻili, his god, standing there.[30] There will be an elevated shelter centered near the bow, where your haku will be sitting, and a shelter astern for the two hoʻokele."

As the two were talking, the sun emerged, and the keiki saw the sides of the aliʻi's canoe shining in the sun's rays and the paddles sparkling as the hoewaʻa lifted them from the water.

The keiki asked, "Perhaps my haku is coming in this canoe?"

"ʻAe, that's right. Your haku should be there—look for him," said Pākaʻa.

"There's my haku approaching us," said Kūapākaʻa.

"Where?" asked Pākaʻa.

"There, seaward of us."

"Raise your paddle straight up, so it can be seen," said Pākaʻa. Pākaʻa's brother Lapakahoe, who was on the aliʻi's canoe, saw the upright paddle and said to the aliʻi, "Ē! There's a small canoe shoreward of us, and someone in it is holding up a paddle. Let's go there."

The hoʻokele asked, "Why are we going toward that upright paddle of a little keiki?"

Keawenuia'umi responded from his shelter: "You two ho'okele want me to ignore the upright paddle. That's the very reason I have to search for Pāka'a. Pāka'a acknowledges the kānaka nui and the kānaka iki, the fleet of canoes and the single canoe—like that little canoe floating there; he acknowledges the person calling out and the person holding up the paddle, because the person may want to say something or offer some 'ai and i'a for our sustenance. Go toward that small canoe; perhaps the keiki has something to say." The ho'okele pointed the canoe toward the spot where the small canoe was floating.

The ali'i ordered the ho'okele to do this because he was accustomed to doing this when he sailed with Pāka'a. When Pāka'a saw a canoe with someone holding a paddle upright, he would tell the ali'i to visit the canoe, perhaps just to say a word.

As the ali'i's canoe was approaching, Pāka'a asked his keiki, "Where is your haku now?"

"Very close by."

"Call out—tell your haku's crew what to do," said Pāka'a, so Kūapāka'a called out:

Hold back on the paddles, hold back,
Be still, be still,
Bring the canoe into the calm, bring it in,
Gently, gently,
Listen to this call,
The query of the question,
I, a keiki, am calling out,
Whose canoe is this?

Some of the crew responded, "The canoe belongs to Keawenuia'umi."

"Where's the canoe going?"

"The canoe is going in search of Pāka'a."

"What is 'Pāka'a'?"

"A kauwā."[31]

Then Kūapāka'a asked his father so the others couldn't hear, "Are you really an ali'i, or are you a kauwā? What of it anyway, even if you are a kauwā. My mother is an ali'i, so I'm an ali'i while I live here on Moloka'i."

Pāka'a whispered back to Kūapāka'a to ask his question again to those

34

on the canoe, so the keiki asked them, "Is Pāka'a really a kauwā?"
"Not a real kauwā," they said. "He holds up the kāhili, carries the
ali'i's ointment calabash, and picks out the ali'i's 'uku."

"You're a high-ranking ali'i who may place his hand on the head of
Keawenuia'umi," Kūapāka'a said to his father. The keiki realized his
father was indeed an important ali'i and added, "Since you're an ali'i and
my mother is an ali'i, I'm an ali'i loa while living here on Moloka'i."

Then Pāka'a ordered the keiki to call out his haku's name, so
Kūapāka'a called out:

The canoe is yours,
Great Hawai'i of Kāne,
Great Hawai'i, land of the sun,
The sun emerges, emerges,
The sun emerges at Ha'eha'e,[32]
With a strong affectionate love for my haku,
Not my real haku,
But a companion of the giddy sun,
The Kona sun without food,
Its loved one has arrived,
Arrived along with Hilo of Kāne,
Hilo of Kāneakapu,
Hilo, land of Kanilehua,
Beloved companion of Keawenuia'umi mā,
There sits Keawenuia'umi,
The canoe is yours.

When Kūapāka'a finished his chant, Kahikuokamoku, the Kuhina Nui,
recited the following chant:

You don't know, keiki,
You don't know the canoe is
For Kū, for Lono,
For Kāne and Kanaloa,[33]
For the forty-thousand gods,
The four-hundred-thousand gods;
The canoe is of the rainy land of Hilo of Malama,
The rain falls,
The misty, sticky rain of Hanakahi,

Gentle and passing is the rain,
Muddy and wet is the sand,
Scattered are the leaves of the forest,
Leleiwi is left standing apart at the sea,
The kapa of Kahulaana is bundled up,
The clouds rise over the hala of Hōpoe,
Quickly reaching Kea'au,
The fish move cautiously at Ki'i,
The canoe is Keawenuia'umi's.

When Kahikuokamoku finished his chant, Kūapāka'a chanted back:

The canoe is yours, O Hilo of the rain,
The rain of Kuhihewa makes a lei,
The rain of Eleao continues to fall,
The rain of Eleao pelts the hala,
Then Hanakahi warms up,
The first calm day for the fisherman,
The fisherman who nets the nehu of Hilo,
Greeting the native of that place,
The old native-born of that place,[34]
The canoe is yours.

The keiki paused; when no one on the ali'i's canoe responded, he chanted again:

The canoe is yours,
The face of Ha'ikū darkens,
Ie-aniani comes from the place of winds,
Where? Windward? Leeward?
The sea rises at the cliffs,
The sea current of the Beloved Friend,
Your loved one, his loved one,
There alone, there alone,
There is Keaweopu,
Sitting there at the seashore,
At sea is your fisherman, O Keawe,
The canoe is yours.

Then the keiki rested, but soon, because Keawenuia'umi's crew
seemed to enjoy his chants, Kūapāka'a called out another one:

So the canoe is yours,
The source of storms has arrived,
The low-hanging clouds are torn,
The gusty, gloomy Lele-uli rain,
The black heads of the clouds,
With a black mantle on the mountain of Aluli,
The face of the Kawaikapu cliffs,
Veering this way and that,
The Holopo'opo'o wind veering this way and that,
Breaking the ferns of the water,
Pulling up the ferns of Mauna,
Waiehu swept by Kapahi,
The trembling noio soars to heaven,
The sound of the grindstone Kuaiwa,
The sound of the mournful grindstone,
Rasping in the rising sea,
Like Kahiwa at Kikipua,
The high officer leaps over the current of Malelewa'a,
Carrying the ukana on the back,
Holding the keiki in front,
Lowering gradually the line from mast to bow,
The Ka'ula wind climbs
The cliffs of Oloku'i,
Cliff joined to cliff at Wailau,
Joined, united are the brows of the cliffs,
Above Pueohulunui, the owl cliff of Aua,
The canoe is yours.[35]

It was a sunny day and because there were women along with the ali'i,
Kūapāka'a chanted concerning the women:

The canoe is yours,
When it rains, the women bundled in kī-leaf rain capes,
Like birds perched in the 'ōhi'a blossoms,
Walk with their legs apart, straddling the path to Mahiki;
The 'Ākōlea rain strikes the hill of water,
Mahiki is slippery in the water and rain,

Mahiki is not slippery when the sun is out,
Mahiki is slippery in the rain
For the feet of the kanaka,
By foot, my travelling and arriving,
When the fish move slowly to Hilo,
At Hilo, the canoe is yours.

The keiki's improvised chant refers to the opening wide of the thighs of women who straddle the path to Mahiki, a place that gets slippery when it rains; thus, he alludes to the women who open their thighs at death in the current in the ocean.[36]

When Kūapāka'a finished chanting, Kahikuokamoku asked, "How did you learn these chants, ē nā keiki?"

"These chants are learned by all the children of this place."

"We're leaving now, so if you have anything more to say, say it now."

"I call on you to bring the canoes ashore. There is a little 'ai from the uplands and some i'a, too. Tomorrow is a calm day for sailing; today will be stormy: there are thick cumulus clouds resting above Kawainui and the ridge of Wailau; when these clouds are blown with full force, a terrible storm will rage; when the clouds are at rest again, then good weather will follow. That's what I have to tell you."[37]

There were no clouds yet—only the clouds in the wind gourd. The keiki was trying to trick them into coming ashore by saying there were cumulus clouds rising at Kawainui.

The ho'okele responded rudely to the keiki: "Maybe the ali'i won't bring the canoe ashore as you asked him to, ē nā keiki, because if your channel is stormy, the ali'i's canoe would be smashed to bits in it. Then we'd have to use your bones to drill holes to lash the ali'i's canoe back together."

Kūapāka'a asked his father without the others hearing, "Ē! Is what they say true?"

"'A'ole."

Pāka'a advised his keiki about how to respond, and Kūapāka'a contradicted them, "Ē! Human bones aren't used to drill holes in a canoe. The stone adze is used to chop down the tree, trim away the top and the side branches, and carve the outside and inside into the right shape. Then pig and dog bones, not human bones, are used to drill holes in the canoe."

All the kānaka in Keawenuia'umi's canoes agreed: "You're right, ē ke keiki. Those two ho'okele were impertinent and presumptuous, puffing

38

themselves up on their own words."

Kahikuokamoku said, "I'm not speaking on behalf of those two, but I have a question: how is it a calm day like today can be a bad day for sailing? The sky is clear, the mountain tops are exposed, and the banks of clouds are asleep at the horizon."

Kūapāka'a said, "This will be a stormy day, a windy day. You came here from Hawai'i with the winds from there; Hawai'i is a windy land, and they blow here from behind you."

The keiki was a kama'āina of this place, the hot, dry coast of Pālā'au mā, where it's calm in the evenings and the mornings, but when noon approaches, the Moa'e blows. As the day grew warmer, he knew the winds of his island would blow very hard, so he predicted the winds would come from behind them.

"How did you learn the winds of Hawai'i? You've probably never been there," said Kahikuokamoku.

"As I told you before, the children of this island amuse themselves by learning chants. I can recite the chant of the winds of the island of Hawai'i, winds to destroy you."

"Begin then."

Kūapāka'a chanted:

Hurry, hurry,
The source of the storms of Hilo,
Is the wind called ua kea,[38]
Shearing off the edges of a hale and breaking it up,
Kēpia is of Hilo of the upright cliffs,
Uluau is of Waiākea,
Ulumano, 'Awa, Pu'ulena,
Moani'ala are of Puna,
The winds of Kuamoa'e have gathered,
My Moa'e, the wind that is swelling,
Apaiahaa is at Kanakaloloa,
Hau is of Kapalilua,
'Eka is of Kona,
Kipu is of Kahuā,
'E'elekoa is of Uli,
Kīpu'upu'u is of Waimea,
'Ōlauniu is of Kekaha,

Pa'ala'a is in the ocean,
Nāulu is of Kawaihae,
A wind that comes
And dashes the milo leaves of Makaopau,
Kalāhuipua'a, 'Āpa'apa'a is of Kohala's upland cliffs,
The wind that flies about like vapor,
Pu'ukolea is of Kapa'au,
Holopo'opo'o is of Waipi'o,
'Aeloa is of Hāmākua,
Kona is the wind of the sky
Above the 'Alenuihāhā sea,
You should come ashore,
The spray of the sea flies up,
The spray of the wind, a storm is coming.

Kahikuokamoku asked, "Are these the only winds of the island of Hawai'i?"

Kūapāka'a said, "'A'ole, here are more." Then he began to chant:

At Ka'ū's windy cape is Ka 'Īlio a Lono,[39]
The paddle is dipped into the sea of Kāiliki'i,
At Puna's foundation turns the sun, the light,
Go and feel the wind of Kumukahi,
Hilo's wind-blown rain at sea,
The rain is seaward, over the hala of Leleiwi,
The spray of rain is at Hāmākua,
Hāmākua is the bridge to the cliffs,
At Kohala-iki is the Moa'e wind, the Moa'e blows,
Kona awakens with the Kēhau breeze,
Kona's burden diminishing with the Kēhau breeze,
Keawenuia'umi, come ashore, a storm is coming.

"Are these all of Hawai'i's winds?" asked Kahikuokamoku.

Kūapāka'a answered, "'A'ole, there are more—but wait. If you agree to come ashore with us, my chanting will be worth my while. But if not, I'm wasting my breath. I told you earlier this will be a stormy day. No ho'okele is skillful enough to get you to O'ahu in the terrible storm that's coming." Kūapāka'a's repudiation of the two ho'okele-wa'a annoyed them greatly.

Kahikuokamoku asked his kāhuna, kilo, and kākā'ōlelo, "Will this really be a stormy day?"

They said, "There won't be a storm. This is a good day for sailing."
The ho'okele urged the ali'i to go on, but the canoe couldn't move forward because Kipukohola was holding back with his paddle; he wanted to stay because he was enjoying the keiki's chants; Kahikuokamoku and Keawenuia'umi also admired the way the keiki expertly chanted, using ancient words like an adult.

Kūapāka'a saw his haku's encouraging look and called out the rest of the winds of Hawai'i in a chant:

There, there are the winds rising from the earth,
The 'Āpa'apa'a is of Kohala,
The rainy wind called Nāulu is of Kawaihae,
The Kīpu'upu'u is of Waimea,
A cold wind that hurts the skin,
A wind that whips the kapa of that land about,
Tossing up dust before it,
Frightening the procession of travelers,
'Ōlauniu is the wind,
Pili-a is of Kanikū,
A'e is of Kala'au,
Pohu and 'Eka are the winds of Kona,
Ma'a'akuulapu is of Kahalu'u,
Pilihala is of Ka'awaloa,
Kēhau is of Kapalilua,
Piuohooilo is of Ka'ū,
Ho'olapa is of Kamā'oa,
Kuehulepo is of Nā'ālehu
Uahipele is of Kīlauea,
'Awa is of Leleiwi,
Pu'ulena is of Waiākea,
Uluau is of Hilo-pali-kū,
Koholālele is of Hāmākua,
Holopo'opo'o is of Waipi'o,
The tip of that wind,
The tip of this wind,
They will twist into a whirlwind,
The bundle of bones at the back of the canoe exhaling,

Breaking off the buoy floating at the front;
Taking the load from the swamped canoe,
The small canoe will be swamped,
Destroyed with the large canoe,
The ali'i will die, the kāhuna will die,
The weak will die, the strong will die,
The dark wisemen, the bright wisemen,
They will search out, they will confer
To locate the stars of the wave,
O Hōkū'ula, O Hōkūlei,[40]
They will swim singly, they will swim by twos,
Yesterday was a calm day,
A crowd of fishermen was at sea,
The paddling of the good canoes,
The strength of the hoewa'a,
The wisdom of the ho'okele,
Don't go far out to sea, ē dear ones,
Stop here, those from Hawai'i,
Come here over the sea surface,
You will be possessed on O'ahu,
There will be darkness only on calm O'ahu,
Yesterday was calm, today will be stormy;
Keawenuia'umi, come ashore, a storm is coming.

Kahikuokamoku answered, "The ali'i's canoes won't go ashore with you, ē ke keiki. These winds you've called out belong to Hawai'i. They blow over the sea of 'Alenuihāhā and die out there. The winds of Hawai'i won't reach here."

Kūapāka'a said, "Since you deny the winds of Hawai'i, here in front of you is O'ahu, another windy land."

Kahikuokamoku said, "Let's hear the names of the O'ahu winds."

Kūapāka'a chanted the winds of O'ahu:

There are our clouds, my father's and mine,
Covering the mountains;
The clouds rise with a sudden shower,
The whirling winds blow,
The source of the storm of the keiki,
Ku a ē-ho is at sea,

From the sea, the storm comes sweeping toward shore,
The windward Kui-lua wind churns up the sea,
While you're fishing and sailing,
The Ihiihilauakea wind blows,
It's the wind that blows inside Hanauma,
A wind from the mountains that darkens the sea,
It's the wind that tosses the kapa of Paukua,
Puuokona is of Kuli'ou'ou,
Ma-ua is the wind of Niu,
Holouhā is of Kekaha,
Māunuunu is of Wai'alae,
The wind of Lē'ahi turns here and there,
'Ōlauniu is of Kahaloa,
Wai'ōma'o is of Pālolo,
Kuehu-lepo is of Kahua,
Kukalahale is of Honolulu,
'Ao'aoa is of Māmala,
'Ōlauniu is of Kapālama,
Haupe'epe'e is of Kalihi,
Ko-momona is of Kahauiki,
Ho'e'o is of Moanalua,
Moa'e-ku is of Ewaloa,
Kēhau is of Waiopua,
Waikōloa is of Līhu'e,
Kona is of Pu'uokapolei,
Māunuunu is of Pu'uloa,
Kaiāulu is of Wai'anae,
Kumuma'oma'o is of Kamaile,
Kumaipo is of Kualele,
Kopiliehu is of Olopua,
The wind of Ka'ena turns in two directions,
Hinakokea is of Mokulē'ia,
The winds of Waialua blow,
Moving silently at the cape of Ka'ena,
Pu'u-ka'ala blows at Ka'ala,
Kēhau is of Kapo,
The sea wind blows hard,
Mālualua comes from the northeast,
Peapueo is of Kaunala,

Ahamanu is of Kahuku,
Lanakila is of Hau'ula,
Moa'e is of Punalu'u,
'Āhiu is of Kahana,
Holopali is of Ka'a'awa and Kualoa,
Kiliua is of Waikāne,
Mololani is of Kua'a'ohe,
Ulumano is of Kāne'ohe,
The wind is for Kaholoakeāhole,
Puahiohio is the upland wind of Nu'uanu,
Malanai is of Kailua,
Limu-li-pu'upu'u comes ashore at Waimānalo,
'Alopali is of Pāhonu,
At Makapu'u the winds turn,
The Kona winds turn, the Ko'olau winds turn,
The winds will turn before you and find you,
You'll be overwhelmed, O deaf ali'i,
The winds will gather,
The na'ena'e leaves will bend,
You'll be swept ashore at Awawamalu,
Caught in the fishing net of the head fisherman,
Your thigh bone and upper-arm bone
Will be made into fishhooks,
To catch the pāo'o and the 'ōpakapaka,
Your flesh will be without bones,
The black crab, the shearwater will eat your remains,
The life from the parents will be broken off,
Here I am, the 'aumakua kanaka,
Listen to my life-giving words,
Keawenuia'umi, come ashore, a storm is coming,
When you sailed yesterday, it was calm.[41]

After the winds of O'ahu had been named, the kānaka were uncertain: they didn't believe fully in the keiki's words, yet they were afraid that he might be right and that some of them might die at sea.

They sat quietly, hoping perhaps the keiki's haku would go ashore; while they waited calmly for something to be said, they just stared fixedly at the keiki's moored canoe.

After a while, Lapakahoe said, "You're really smart, little keiki, and your chanting is delightful. Your memorizing of the chants of the winds of Hawai'i and O'ahu is extraordinary! Are these the only windy lands?"

"'A'ole, Kaua'i is also a windy land."

"Do you know the names of Kaua'i's winds?"

"'Ae." Then Kūapāka'a called out the winds of Kaua'i as follows:

There, see the wind,
A wind, the wind gourd of La'amaomao,
The Kiu, the Ko'olauwahine breeze, where I left it,
Calling out to the multitudes, to the row of mountains,
A cloud sign of the scattering wind,
A cloud formed by winds gathering at Kapa'a,
There they are, the winds of Kaua'i,
Moa'e is of Lehua,
Mikioi is of Kawaihoa,
Nāulu is of Ni'ihau,
Ko'olau is of Kaulakahi,
Lawakua is of Nāpali
Lani-ku'u-wa'a is of Kalalau,
Lauae is of Honopū,
'Aiko'o is of Nu'alolo,
Kuehu-kai is the wind of Miloli'i,
Pu'ukapele is of Mānā,
Moeahua is of Kekaha,
Waipao is of Waimea,
Kapaahoa is of Kahana,
Makaupili is of Pe'ape'a,
Aoao is of Hanapēpē,
Unulau is of Wahiawā,
Kiuanu is of Kalāheo,
A'e is of Lāwa'i,
Malanai is of Kōloa,
Ku'iamanini is of Weliweli,
Makahuena is of Pā'ā,
Onehali is of Manenene,
Ko'omakani is of Māhā'ulepū,
Paupua is of Kīpū,
Ala'oli is of Hulē'ia,
Waikai is of Kalapakī,

Kāʻao is of Hanamāʻulu,
Waipuaʻaʻala is the wind
That knocks down hale of Konolea,
Waiʻōpua is of Wailua,
Waiolohia is of Nahanahanai,
Inuwai is of Waipouli,
Hoʻolua is the wind of Makaīwa,
Kēhau is of Kapaʻa,
Malamalamamaikai is of Keālia,
Hulilua is of Hōmaikawaʻa,
Amu is of Anahola,
Kololio is of Moloaʻa,
Kiukainui is of Koʻolau,
Maheu is of Kalihiwai,
Nau is of Kalihikai,
Lūhau is of Hanalei,
Waiamau is of Waiʻoli,
Puʻunahele is of Waipā,
Haukoloa is of Lumahaʻi,
Lūpua is of Wainiha,
Pahelehala is of Naue,
Limahuli is of Hāʻena.
Near the waterfall at the cliff,
The water trickling down the paddle handle
To quench one's thirst,
The tip of that wind,
The tip of this wind,
They'll twist into a whirlwind,
Rushing out over the sea.
Come ashore, a storm is coming, yesterday was calm.
Here are ʻai from the upland, iʻa, kapa, malo;
If you sail over the ocean,
Remember the keiki who hasn't come with you,
The outgoing and incoming currents will carry you,
Possessed there at Hanauma,
You will be caught by fishermen,
Carried to the harmful spirit,[42]
You'll be called a castaway,

Turn toward my sun and live,
You deaf ali'i of Hawai'i,
Come ashore, a storm is coming,
Tomorrow will be calm.

When the chant ended, Kahikuokamoku said, "So a storm will strike today, ē ke keiki?"

Kūapāka'a said, "'Ae, today will be stormy. The wind will rise from the cape of Kawaihoa, Ni'ihau, and turn back the bow of your canoe." The ali'i's crew didn't respond. While they were calmly floating without saying anything, they heard thunder and a roaring of wind.

Then Pāka'a told the keiki, "You blundered when you called out Kaua'i's winds because you began with Hawai'i's winds, which are the easternmost winds. You should then call out Ka'ula's wind, which is the westernmost wind, not of Kaua'i." So Kūapāka'a called out for Ka'ula's wind:

There, there, there below the rock of Ola
The black bird begged
The bird of Ka'ula begged
Suspended there above Wa'ahila
The bird of Ka'ula-naula
The favorite young island, given birth by Hina,
Ekeu-ekeu is the wind of Ka'ula
Bring here, bring here the wind.[43]

Keawenuia'umi told Kūapāka'a, "Your chanting is delightful, ē ke keiki, but you blundered when you called for a wind. I told you I'm searching for my kahu, Pāka'a, and you called out, 'Bring here, bring here the wind,' so now that a wind is coming I won't come ashore with you."

He told Ho'okele-i-Hilo and Ho'okele-i-Puna, "Let's go."

The kānaka readied their paddles to go as their ali'i had ordered, but Lapakahoe didn't want to go because he was fascinated by the keiki's chanting, so when the kānaka in the middle and astern began to paddle, Lapakahoe quickly ordered the kānaka toward the bow—Kuia, Lona and Kipukohola, to hold back on their paddles to prevent the canoe from moving. The pebbles stirred, and the sand scattered on the sea bottom beneath the canoe, but the canoe remained in the same place, as if it were anchored.

Kūapāka'a looked at Lapakahoe, then said to Pāka'a, "The ho'okele ordered the kānaka to paddle, but some of them are holding back with their paddles, so the canoe is stalled."

Keawenuiaʻumi was getting very angry at the keiki and commanded the kānaka to paddle. Kūapākaʻa told his father, "The aliʻi is very angry with me and has shouted at the hoewaʻa to paddle on."

His father said, "Chant," so the keiki chanted:

Hurry! hurry!! hurry!!!
The sky is oppressive,
The earth is distressed,
Harmful spirits in the light,
The mischievous ones rise,
The mischievous ones tarry,
The ʻiwa is aloft,
It's a windy day, it's going to rain,
The water flows, the ʻōpae surface,
The rocks are exposed;
Where the sea rages, the moi remains,
Where the sea spurts, the ʻanae spawns,
Where the tide is low, the pūloa is struck,
The pākiʻi is stepped on, the ʻulae is trampled,
The ʻina is pried up, the wana is hooked,
The honu comes up for air on a windy day,
Where the tide rises, the manini remains,
Where the shoals are rocky, the uoa turns over,
Where the sea is blue, the manō swims,
At the deep-sea fishing grounds, kāhala is hooked,
Where chewed kukui nut is spit to calm the sea,
The uhu is netted,
Caught by those in front, silently, noisily,
The rain borne on the Mālua wind falls,
The winds turn over,
Haualialia of Kaunakakai,
Ihuanu of Kawela,
Akani at Wāwāʻia,
Pohaku-kupukupu at Kamalō,
Reaching Kalaʻe Loa of Lehua,
ʻUalapuʻe, a step away
From Kaluaʻaha and Mapulehu.[44]

48

\When the keiki finished this chant urging quick action, his father
ordered him to chant again, so he did so:

The cloud bank settles in the sky,
The rain water relieves the birth-pains of the clouds,
The black shining rain of Kāne,
The navel of the rain forms in the sky,
The streams swell with the rain,
The thunder roars, the earth rumbles,
The lightning flashes in the sky,
The light rain, the heavy rain,
The long rain, the short rain,
The softly blown rain, the sleep of the rainy season,
The breath is held, the hair is drenched,
The hair is parted in the middle,
Sleep curled up, sleep facing up,
Sleep and obey, sleep and wake up,
The teeth gnash angrily, the hands are slow,
The stubborn haku will die,
The stubborn hoewaʻa, the stubborn hoʻokele
Will die at sea,
You'll leave and be beset by a storm,
You'll be called a castaway,
The fragrance of the imu,
Like a fish hooked, you'll be cut up with shark-teeth,
Your bones will be made into fishhooks,
The olonā twisted to make fishing line, the fish will bite,
The ʻōpakapaka, hapuʻu, ulua,
The month is Kaulua,[45]
Care for the favorite keiki,
Or he'll be lost in the sea of Kaulua,
The canoe should come ashore,
Here are ʻai from the upland, iʻa, kapa, malo,
Stormy days will come before calm seas,
So come ashore, my haku,
Today will be stormy, yesterday was calm.

When the aliʻi heard the voice of the keiki again saying, "It'll be a

49

stormy day," his anger subsided, and he asked his hoʻokele, kāhuna, kilo, and other advisers, "How is it? Should we go ashore as the keiki says?" They responded, "Why should we go ashore here?"

Lapakahoe had paid close attention as Kūapākaʻa named the winds in his chants, and his love for Pākaʻa welled up in his heart, for the keiki's chanting was like the chanting he and Pākaʻa had once done. Lapakahoe asked Kūapākaʻa, "Ē ke keiki, who taught you these chants?"

Kūapākaʻa answered, "I told you earlier I learned them during my childhood on Molokaʻi."

Lapakahoe replied, "Only two people know these chants—my older brother Pākaʻa and I. We composed these chants for our aliʻi, Keawenuiaʻumi. No one else knows them, not even Kahikuokamoku, the aikāne punahele of the aliʻi. Now I hear you reciting the chants, you small little boy. How did you learn them?"

Kūapākaʻa said, "I told you I learned them during my childhood on this island. If you come ashore, you would hear all the children reciting them."

Then Lapakahoe replied, "No one else knows them, only Pākaʻa and I. If what you say is true, Pākaʻa must have taught them to the children. Tell me, do you know if Pākaʻa is living here?"

"No one by that name lives here—we heard that Pākaʻa is on Kaʻula."

Lapakahoe stopped questioning the keiki because he remembered Keawenuiaʻumi had told him that Pākaʻa's spirit had appeared in a dream and said Pākaʻa was on Kaʻula.

Kahikuokamoku saw someone hunched over at the bow of the keiki's canoe and asked, "Who is that at the bow of your canoe?"

"That's my father—he's deaf. He enjoys fishing for uhu."

When Lapakahoe wondered if Pākaʻa was on Molokaʻi, Pākaʻa hoped the aliʻi would go ashore and search for him. Then Pākaʻa could carry out his plan of revenge and end his separation from his hānai. But he didn't want to be discovered right away before his plan unfolded, so when Kahikuokamoku asked, "Who is that at the bow of your canoe?" Pākaʻa worried that he would be discovered. He was afraid that he and his keiki would be ordered to paddle closer, so the aliʻi could ask questions about Pākaʻa's whereabouts. But this danger passed because of the keiki's quick answer: if the old man was deaf, what was the point of questioning him? Thus Pākaʻa escaped detection.

When Kūapākaʻa's exchange with Kahikuokamoku ended, Pākaʻa

ordered the keiki to chant again, so he chanted:

Hurry, hurry, hurry,
The rain, the storm, the winds are coming,
The Puʻulenalena of Hilo, indeed,
Of Koha-i-nae, Hōkūkano, Waiolomea,
The paddles are seized in the starboard hull,
At the thought of running aground,
At the inboard part of the outrigger boom,
At the forward outrigger boom,
At the stern outrigger boom,
At the hollow of the canoe for the hoʻokele,
The buttocks will bestir, the paddles will be lifted,
The anchor pulled up, the waves watched for,
The twisting, the collapsing, the waves of the inside,
The rolling of waves, the paddling outside,
The calm at the canoe's bow, the rolling,
The canoe rolls and stops,
The water outside gathers at the opening,
The beloved canoe hulls of those storm-beset,
Here I am to destroy you!
The small wave will destroy you,
The large wave will destroy you,
The long wave will destroy you,
The short wave will destroy you,
A wave crashing down on the unprepared canoe
Shows that the hoʻokele are unskillful,
The following waves inside, outside,
The roaring, the trembling,
The large wave, the long wave,
The waves that overwhelm,
The waves that overwhelm and swamp your canoe,
The swamping of the small canoes,
The swamping of the large canoes,
The paddles are bound together,
The ukana of a swamped canoe,
The small paddle, the large paddle,
The long paddle, the short paddle,

The small bailing cup, the large bailing cup,
The long bailing cup, the short bailing cup,
The thick bailing cup, the thin bailing cup,
The incompetent ones of the swamped canoe will die,
Trying to refloat the canoe,
That block of wood, this block of wood,
That rope is pulled, this rope is pulled,
That multitude leaves, this multitude leaves,
The large waves rise, the small waves break,
The bow pieces snap off,
The stern pieces snap off,
The kāhuna are sundered,
Rigid with fear and hollow, the pair with no rights,
This is their day of death,
The ocean gapes open, the louse eggs are cold,
The lice are soaked, the wrong-doers are drenched,
You hoʻokele and kilo are disgraced,
The kāhuna and other experts are disgraced,
Look, you two hoʻokele,
For the star of the land, come ashore.

Keawenuiaʻumi was uncertain about what to do, so he again asked his hoʻokele, kāhuna, kilo, and other advisers to look at the signs again to see if the weather would remain good or not because he was afraid that the keiki's words were true, that the weather would turn bad. He wanted to know if they would die at sea if they didn't go ashore, as Kūapākaʻa had predicted.

So the aliʻi asked again, "What shall we do? Go ashore as the keiki says?"

The advisers responded, "'Aʻole, there's no storm coming—the keiki is wahaheʻe—a liar. Where are the clouds? Where are the cloud banks? Where is the rain? Where is the wind? Where is the thunder? Where is the lightning? What makes you think the keiki is telling the truth? This is your day to sail to Kaʻula, where you'll find your kauwā, Pākaʻa."

When the keiki heard them call him wahaheʻe, he calmly told his father, "The advisers refuse to land here."

His father said, "Improvise another chant," so Kūapākaʻa chanted again:

The eyes are blinded by the sea spray,
Which hides the line of islands,
These are the days of Kū
When the current flows outward,
The current enters the depths of the sea,
The mouth of the manō gapes open,
To snatch you up, Keawenuia'umi,
You'll return only in spirit to Hawai'i;
O deaf ali'i, come ashore, a storm is coming,
Tomorrow will be calm.

Then the ali'i again asked the ho'okele and kāhuna, "Shall we go ashore as the keiki advises? If we sail on, he says only our spirits will return to Hawai'i."

The ho'okele and the kāhuna said to the ali'i, "We won't go ashore— this is a calm day and that keiki is wahahe'e." Then the ho'okele chanted to Kūapāka'a:

Who will go ashore on a calm day?
The heavens are cloudless, the shrubs are dry,
The clouds have gone back to the mountains,
The wind has gone back to Kumukahi,
The cloud banks have gone back to 'Awalau,
The gloomy wind-blown showers have gone back,
The canoes have gone back
To the deepening rough-water channel,
The canoes have gone back to the windy cape,
The sea has gone back, the water of Manawainui,
Where is your storm today, ē nā keiki?

Kūapāka'a chanted back:

There is our fish, my father's and mine,
A hīnālea returns to the cave,
Bunched up, curled up in the storm;
There is our uhu, my father's and mine,
Coming to the edge of the net,
Baring their teeth, showing their teeth in anger,

53

There is our coconut, my father's and mine,
Planted in the ocean, growing in the ocean,
Bearing fruit in the ocean, ripening in the ocean,
The voice of the coconut is a creaking,
Creaking in the storm.[46]

The ho'okele said, "Your tongue is as slippery as a he'e, ē nā keiki. Who planted this coconut in the ocean, so that it sprouted, grew, bore fruit, and ripened in the sea?"

Kūapāka'a said, "The head, where the ears stand up, didn't pay attention."

Kahikuokamoku said, "'Ae, is the creaking of the sennit of our canoe your coconut's voice?"

Kūapāka'a said, "That's the coconut's voice—the lashings of your canoe are made of twisted coconut-husk fibers. This answers the riddle, 'What coconut grows in the ocean?'"

The two ho'okele were offended by the keiki's wit, so Ho'okele-i-Hilo responded, "You're a nobody, ē nā keiki, but your words are very annoying. We'll sail to O'ahu, and when we come back, we'll roast you in an imu."

The keiki whispered to his father, "Is what he says true?"

Pāka'a advised the keiki, and Kūapāka'a responded, "You won't kill me—you'll die at sea before that."

The talking stopped while the crew prepared to go. When they began to paddle away, the keiki told his father, "My haku is about to go."

Pāka'a replied, "Call out the winds of Maui and Moloka'i"; so Kūapāka'a called out:

There, there, the windy clouds rest,
The Paliale is Hilo's wind,
Pāki'ele is of Waiākea,
Hāna's winds are 'Ai-maunu,
Kaomi, Kāpae,
Ho'olua, Lauawaawa,
Paiolopaowa, Halemauu,
Kui, Kona;
Koholā-pehu is of Kīpahulu,
Koholā-lele as well,
'Ai-loli is of Kaupō,

54

Moaʻe is of Kahikinui,
Papa is of Honuaʻula,
Nāulu is at Kanaloa,
Hau descends from the uplands of Kula,
It's the wind of that place,
Searching the pili,
Nau is the wind of Kula,
ʻUlalena is at Piʻiholo,
ʻŪkiu is of Makawao,
The Puukoa rain is at Kokomo,
The Elehei rain is at Lilikoʻi,
The gentle, cool rain there,
Haule-aku is at Mauoni,
Hau-aku is at Keālia,
Kaumuku is of Papawai,
Olaukoa is at Ukumehame,
The wind that tears apart the hale at Olowalu,
Kilihau is the rain there,
Kololio is of Waikapū,
Iʻa-iki is of Wailuku,
ʻOʻopu is of Waiheʻe,
The Kauaʻula wind blows,
Roaring up the cliffs,
The cliffs of Kahakuloa,
Of Waiuli at Honolua,
Pohakea is at Māhinahina,
Līlīlehua is at the cliffs,
ʻImihau is of Kekaʻa,
Nahua is at Kāʻanapali,
Unuloa fills the sail,
Maʻaʻa is of Lahaina,
Settling at Kamaiki,
Moaʻeaʻe-aku is at the cliffs,
Alani is of Liloa,
Paʻalā is of Kaha,
The children of Ku and Naiwi,
Kaiāulu is at Pulupulu,
Holio is on the plains,
Holio is the wind,

Laukoaie is on the plains,
Holo-kaomi is at Paomaʻi,
The wind that doubles up is of the lowlands,
Kupa and Okea are the winds,
Paiolua is of the ocean,
Hoʻolua, Moaʻe,
Kaʻele are at Pālāʻau,
Haualialia is there,
Laumaomao is at Punakou,
Lawelawe-malie is at Kekaha,
Haleolono is at Kaluakoʻi,
The Iki-aea is at Hoʻolehua,
The Kuapa is at Moʻomomi,
The Kiola-kapa wind of Kaeleawaa,
Waikaloa is the wind
At Puʻupāpaʻi, Puʻuanahulu, Kaʻamola,
The wind that buffets the canoes of Molokaʻi,
Makaolehua at Kaluaʻaha,
The Puʻu-lolo at Mapulehu,
Puʻu-makani at ʻAhaʻino,
Pakaikai is the wind that blows at Wailua,
Hoʻolua is at Hālawa,
Hoʻolua-noe is at Hālawa,
Hoʻolua-kele is at Hālawa,
Hoʻolua-pehu is at Hālawa,
Hoʻolua-kaʻipou is at Hālawa,
Hoʻolua-wahakole is at Hālawa,
Hikipua is at Hālawa,
Hakaano is at Hālawa,
Laukamani is at Hālawa,
Puʻuohoku is at Hālawa,
Okia is at Hālawa,
Ualehu is at Hālawa,
Laiku is at Hālawa,
Nāulu is at Hālawa,
Kēhau is at Hālawa,
Koipali is at Hālawa,
Līanu is at Hālawa,
ʻEhukai is at Hālawa,

Hauali'ali'a is of Kaunakakai,
Pai is of Kamiloloa,
Ihuanu is of Kawela,
Ekahanui is of Kamalō,
Akani is of Wāwā'ia,
Pohakupukupu is of Ka'amola,
Heakai is of Kalaeloa,
Makaolehua is of Ualapu'e,
Kipukaholo is of Kalua'aha,
Waikōloa is of Mapulehu,
Hukipepeiao is of Kūpeke,
Launahelehele is of Honomuni,
Mauna-i-heleia is of Kainalu,
Kēhau is of Waialua,
Alopali is of Honouli,
Puuohoku is of Moakea,
Kololio is of Keōpuka,
Ho'olua is of Halawa-nui,
Lau-kamani is of Hālawa-iki,
Ho'olua-puakakalo is of Kaahakualua,
Kaaki is of Pāpala-loko,
Leia is of Kikipua,
Ekepue is of Wailau,
Pu'upilo is of Pelekunu,
Kili'o'opu is of Makaluhau,
Kaupu-moa-ula is of Kalawao,
Koki-lae is of Kalaupapa,
Drink the water of birth in the uplands,
Makakuapo is of Nihoa,
Aikupala is of Kahanui,
Noe-ka-maile brings calm,
Kumuma'oma'o is of Kaluako'i,
Ho'olua is that Moa'e bringing clouds,
Ho'olua is this Moa'e bringing clouds,
Turning at Kalā'au cape,
'Ūkiukiu is of Kalama'ula,
Making a new path there,
Burning the 'ai of that hot plain,
Pa'ū-pili brings calm to Īloli,

Striking the sea at low tide
When the i'a are gathered,
The burden of the Moa'e wind,
The Moa'e stays in the uplands,
The Moa'e is at Kona,
Ho'olua is at Ko'olau,
We float in the calm,
At the cape of Kalā'au, the wind turns,
The deep hole foams up,
Koa is of Mālei,
It blows here and there on the coral reef,
Mālualua is of Hale-o-Lono,
Kumuma'oma'o is the Ho'olua in the forest,
A roaring wind of Kona and Ko'olau,
The Ko'olau winds will bring you to the channel-edge,
The small canoes will be swamped,
Destroyed along with the large canoes,
The genitals will be dulled, the scrotums will shrivel up,
The ho'okele will be disgraced,
The kāhuna will be disgraced,
The expert readers of storm signs,
That appear and persist,
That float and persist,
The small ukana, the large ukana,
The bailing cups carelessly left behind,
You'll come to rest on the shore of Hanauma,
The kānaka with the long thighs,
The kānaka with the short thighs,
The fisherman of Kookoo-na-moku,
Crabs will tread on your teeth, and sleep,
The deaf ali'i's life will be ended by the storm,
Ah! Come ashore through the channel,
While you're near, the haku,
While I'm near, the kauwā,
Await the calm day
For this is Welehu, the stormy month,
Makali'i, Kā'elo, Kaulua,
A red glow bursts forth,

In Nana the sea is calm,
Welo and Ikiiki[47]
Are when the fishermen's lines are wet,
Look how the ocean is far,
The island is near,
Bring the canoe ashore,
Search for Pāka'a, find Pāka'a,
Papai, Waimea, Moloka'i are stormy.

As he neared the end of the chant, Kūapāka'a thought that if he hinted Pāka'a was on Moloka'i, he could lure Keawenuia'umi ashore, so he had added the lines:

Bring the canoe ashore,
Search for Pāka'a, find Pāka'a.

When Lapakahoe heard this, he said to Kūapāka'a, "You chanted very beautifully, but you're lying now. Earlier I asked you about Pāka'a, and you said you didn't know about him. Now in this chant, you say, 'Search for Pāka'a, find Pāka'a.' I think you're lying."

Lapakahoe was angry, so he called on the hoewa'a and the ho'okele to go, and they quickly prepared to leave.

Kūapāka'a said to his father, "My haku is going. The kānaka are ready with their paddles and have taken their seats."

Pāka'a said, "Call out the names of the hoewa'a and your haku. Perhaps if they hear their names called out, they'll agree to beach the canoes and depart tomorrow instead."

Kūapāka'a stood up, and before the hoewa'a of the ali'i could dip their paddles into the sea, he called out loudly:

Hurry! Hurry!! Hurry!!!
Hasten! Hasten!! Hasten!!!
Be prepared, be ready,
That canoe, this canoe,
Hands working together, grabbing the paddles,
The sea is calm,
The wet and cold are ended,
Let the backbone and side be slippery,
Move, those seated in front and back,
Like chopping wood,

Firm are the hands while paddling,
The paddle is the burden of the hand,
The wave is the opponent,
The black is laid down,
The white is brought up,
The pieces connecting the hulls are washed over,
The paddles whirl,
Inside, outside, outside, inside,
The canoe begins to move,
Rocking, shaking, dizzying,
The kānaka on the canoe fall down,
The bailing cups knock about,
The 'ōhi'a wood rattles,
The lau hala sails crackles,
The opponent of the wind,
The bow of the canoe dips below,
Who is the kanaka at the bow?

Pāka'a told his keiki, "Lapakahoe, my younger brother." Then Kūapāka'a called out the names of the hoewa'a:

Lapakahoe, who's next?
Lapanaiwiaoao, who's next?
Hookahikuamoo, who's next?
Aohelimakainui, who's next?
Kamahuakoaie, who's next?
Kipukohola, who's next?
Kaili, the god, who's next?
Ku ana Hepa, a kahuna, who's next?
Noho ana Hepa, a kahuna, who's next?
Kauilaokahoeikalima, who's next?
Kaneheakapoohiwi, who's next?
Kahaluluakoaie, who's next?
Mokukaiiakapuhi, who's next?
Ahuakaiiaiwa, who's next?
Uluakamoanaiakaiehu, who's next?
Oaiwaenakahoealiua, who's next?
Halawaimekamakani, who's next?
Hamamakawahaokaalemeheipula, who's next?

Uakukapaiakalailalo, who's next?
Uahaihaikakaoka, who's next?
Uanahaekaioewa, who's next?
Oiukamaewa, who's next?
Okioiokekahuna, who's next?
Kamoeneikawaaokealii, who's next?
Kekioneikaliuwaena, who's next?
The port hull is complete,
The starboard hull is complete,
A query, a question, who are the others?

Kahikuokamoku said, "You've named everyone in this canoe hull. But you haven't named the kānaka in the other hull."

The hoewaʻa in the other hull sat two or three at a seat, one paddling on one side, another on the other side. When one got tired and sore at the outside, he would exchange places with the person on the inside.

After Kahikuokamoku pointed out that the names of the people in the second canoe hull hadn't been called out, Kūapākaʻa continued:

Hurry! Hurry!! Hurry!!!
Sail quickly! Sail quickly!! Sail quickly!!!
Swim there, swim here,
Harmful spirits in the light,
The mischievous ones rise,
The mischievous ones tarry,
The ʻiwa is aloft,
It's a windy day, it's going to rain,
The water flows, the ʻōpae surface,
The rocks are exposed;
Where the sea rages, the moi remains,
Where the sea spurts, the ʻanae spawns,
Where the tide is low, the pūloa is struck,
The pākiʻi is stepped on, the ʻulae is trampled,
The ʻina is pried up, the wana is hooked,
The honu comes up for air on a windy day,
Where the tide rises, the manini remains,
Where the shoals are rocky, the uoa turns over,
Where the sea is blue, the manō swims,
At the deep-sea fishing grounds, kāhala is hooked,

Where chewed kukui nut is spit to calm the sea,
The uhu is netted,
Kui and Lau, a pair, who's next?
Koaloa and Koapoko, a pair, who's next?
Nanaimua and Nanaihope, a pair, who's next?
Puipui, Uhauhali, a pair, who's next?
Neneimua, Neneihope, a pair, who's next?
Kahaneeaku, Kahaneemai, a pair, who's next?
Ku, Ka, a pair, who's next?
Kapilikua, Kapilialo, a pair, who's next?
Kapohina, Kapoae, a pair, who's next?
Kaukaiwahelamakani, Puupuukoaikainei, a pair, who's next?
Hulihana, Hailawakua, a pair, who's next?
Nulani and Haakoa, kāhuna, a pair, who's next?
The slaves Pulale, Makaukau, a pair, who's next?
Keawenuia'umi, Kahikuokamoku, Kīauau, three of them, who's next?
The kānaka at the stern of the canoe,
Ho'okele-i-Hilo and Ho'okele-i-Puna, a pair,
The kānaka at the bow of the canoe,
Kuia and Lona, a pair,
The port hull is complete,
The starboard hull is complete,
Just a query, a question:
What are the names of the people remaining?

Kahikuokamoku answered, "No names remain—you've recited them all. You know our names, but we don't know your name. What is your name?"

"I didn't tell you my name," said Kūapāka'a. "If you agree to come ashore, I'll tell you my name."

Ho'okele-i-Hilo said, "You withhold your name, you deceitful keiki, so you can get us to do what you want. But the ali'i won't go ashore with you. We plan to leave." Then the kānaka began to paddle the canoe away.

The keiki sat down and said to his father, "My haku won't come ashore. My mouth's exhausted from urging your deaf ali'i to come ashore."

"Patience," Pāka'a said. "If he listens, he'll live; if not, he'll die. Your

haku will return because he'll die in the storm if he doesn't listen to you."
The two watched calmly, as the ali'i's canoe headed toward O'ahu; in no time, it was almost out of sight.

Then Pāka'a asked the keiki, "Where is your haku's canoe?"

"The canoe and the kānaka are almost out of sight—I can see only their sail."

Pāka'a said, "Open the wind gourd of La'amaomao."

Kūapāka'a uncovered the gourd and chanted to the winds:

Ē winds that I've called,
Blow here, those of Ka'ula and Kaua'i first,
Those of O'ahu and Hawai'i from the sides,
Those of Maui and Moloka'i last,
Blow true, and overtake the canoe fleet
Of Keawenuia'umi, the ali'i.

When the chant ended, banks of clouds rose, storm clouds flew overhead, the skies darkened, lightning flashed, thunder roared, rain pelted down, and blustery winds blew—a terrible storm!

When Keawenuia'umi saw the storm coming, he remembered the words of the keiki and spoke angrily to his kāhuna, kilo, ho'okele and other experts: "Kā! You dismissed the keiki's words. The keiki said 'It'll be a stormy day,' but you said "A'ole, it'll be a good day, no signs of a storm.' Here are signs of a storm—fire blazing in the sky, thunder rolling, Kulanihakoi spilling over,[48] the wind blowing strongly. What a storm! We're doomed because of you, you ignorant fools! Two or three times I asked you for your advice, but it turns out you don't know anything. The keiki told us to go ashore, and you said his words were wahahe'e. Now I know the keiki was right, and you were wahahe'e. Let's go ashore."

The ali'i's double-hulled canoe had not yet been taken by the storm; the forward canoes with the district ali'i and their kānaka were overwhelmed first, because the first winds blew from the west. The canoes at the front of the fleet, passing off of Kaluahole,[49] were caught by the storm and swamped. When the kānaka tried to swim, they were swept away in the outgoing and ingoing currents and lost at sea. The small canoes were lost in the waves whipped up by the multitude of winds blowing from the front, the back, the sides. When the large canoes went to refloat the swamped small canoes, the large canoes failed; all the canoes

63

were damaged.

Thus the destruction continued until the double-hulled canoe of Keawenuia'umi was also caught and swamped, floating helplessly among the waves. All the canoes were swamped, and the survivors were cold and shivering from the rain and the sea. Their bodies were going into shock from the cold. Most of the supplies—the 'ai, the i'a, the kapa, and other necessities—were lost.

The ali'i wept from the cold and again scolded his ho'okele, kāhuna, kilo, and other experts for their foolish advice: "I wanted to find Pāka'a— you blundered, no knowledge, no skill. These buttocks wouldn't be wet if Pāka'a were here. Because of your incomptence, I'm soaked to the bone. I may even die here at sea."

In the strong wind and the pounding seas, he called in vain for the experts at refloating swamped canoes.

Pāka'a watched the storm's devastation from his canoe, then told his keiki, "Cover your gourd so your ali'i won't suffer from the cold." Kūapāka'a covered the wind gourd and the sea became calm. In no time the storm had passed, and the sun came out and warmed the ocean. The biggest canoes, belonging to Keawenuia'umi and the district ali'i, were still partially afloat. The crews bailed the canoes and climbed back into them. When the ali'i got back into his canoe, he looked around for land and saw that O'ahu and Lāna'i were far away. Moloka'i was the closest island, so he decided to go back there. "Perhaps we'll find the keiki who was anchored there. If he urges us to land again, this time we'll land."

Kahikuokamoku and the rest of the kānaka agreed, so the fleet went back to Moloka'i. The canoes were paddled so they would arrive before nightfall at the place where they met the keiki. It was already getting dark. Keawenuia'umi's hoewa'a were the strongest, so his canoe moved into the lead, with the rest of the canoes falling behind. The ali'i's canoe was the first one Kūapāka'a saw returning.

The keiki told his father, "Here comes my haku now."

"Where?" asked Pāka'a.

"There."

Pāka'a told the keiki, "If your haku tries to enter the harbor, tell him that the channel is dangerously crooked and that you and I will go ahead to guide his canoe; when we reach a safe spot, we'll signal for his canoe to follow. We'll lead the way to shore and his canoe will follow us. If we let them go ashore on their own, they'll land before us and I'll be discovered."

When the ali'i's canoe was nearby, Kūapāka'a called out:

Hurry! Hurry!! Hurry!!!
The rain comes with the wind, the island is dark,
The haku comes quietly,
The rain twisted, the canoes rolled,
The sea raged, the puna coral flew up,
The crew slipped down, eaten by the waves,
The ukana on the canoe,
And the canoe itself were tossed up,
The wind challenged the loved ones of the keiki,
Wept for the loved ones of the women,
Keawenuia'umi sat in the hale,
The seat was stormy, unsteady,
The 'īlio in the sea snapped angrily,
Bit the bow of the canoe,
The expert ho'okele,
The companion in front was made to crawl,
The companion in back departed,
The companion of the kāhuna took over,
Bowed his head with humility, trembled,
Grew bewildered, shivered,
The body hair bristled in fright as they sailed,
You, Keawenuia'umi-a-Līloa.

Keawenuia'umi said, "'Ae, you were right, ē ke keiki. What you predicted turned out to be true. Now I'm going to come ashore as you suggested. I thought my ho'okele-wa'a knew what they were talking about, but they didn't."

"Now you know the danger of not coming ashore through the keiki's channel?"

"'Ae, let's go ashore," said Keawenuia'umi.

Then Kūapāka'a replied: "Ē! Listen, ē ke ali'i, we two will go first while you wait behind. When we beckon you with our hands, you follow us. The channel zigzags. The time is past for going ashore unguided. If you had listened to me earlier and come ashore when the tide was low, you would have been able to see the coral heads. Now that the tide is high, you can't see them. You won't know which way to go and if your canoe hits the reef, it'll be badly damaged. Then when good weather returns, you won't have a canoe to search for Pāka'a and return to Hawai'i."

The ali'i said, "'Ae, you're right, ē ke keiki. We'll follow you to shore." The keiki pulled up the stone anchor and placed it on board his father's canoe, then he and his father paddled ahead to a safe deep spot and stopped. Kūapāka'a signaled, and Keawenuia'umi mā followed. When the ali'i reached the safe spot, the small canoe went forward again. That's how they entered the harbor, zigzagging in among the coral heads. Near shore Kūapāka'a paddled vigorously and landed on the sandy beach.

As soon as the bow of the canoe touched the sand, Pāka'a jumped off and ran into a hale 'ā'īpu'upu'u, which he and his keiki had stocked with food. Pāka'a knew he could hide there from his ali'i because only 'ā'īpu'upu'u would ever enter such a hale.

When Pāka'a leaped from the canoe and ran into the hale, Lapakahoe saw him from the bow of the ali'i's canoe and thought the kanaka looked very much like Pāka'a because the kanaka limped as Pāka'a did; but he doubted himself because he believed Pāka'a was on Ka'ula.

By evening, all the canoes had landed, but Keawenuia'umi remained on the platform of his double-hulled canoe because he had no dry kapa or malo to wear since all his clothing had been lost at sea. Kūapāka'a saw his haku shivering on the canoe, so he went to speak to his father: "I pity my haku because he's suffering from the cold. He just sits there in a wet malo on the canoe, without any kapa covering."

Pāka'a took out one of Keawenuia'umi's malo which he had cared for when he was the ali'i's kahu; he gave it to his keiki: "Here's one of your haku's malo. Take it to him. Ask him to remove the wet malo he's wearing and bring it back here. Tell him that this malo you give him is yours."

Kūapāka'a took the dry malo and offered it to Keawenuia'umi saying, "Here's my insignificant malo for you. Please remove your wet one."

Keawenuia'umi gave his wet malo to Kūapāka'a, and the keiki gave the ali'i the dry one. Keawenuia'umi noticed the dry malo looked very much like one of his own. He said to Kūapāka'a, "Perhaps this is one of my malo—it looks like one of mine."

The keiki said, "The malo is mine. My mother beat the kapa for it and was saving it until I could wear it in public as an adult. But now it's yours, my haku."

After the ali'i had taken off his wet malo and put on the dry one, he placed the wet one in the keiki's care.

The keiki returned with it and when he reached the door of Pāka'a's hale, his father asked him, "Where is your haku's malo?"

"Here it is."

"Hang it at the door of my hale, so that the 'ā'īpu'upu'u can no longer come in here."

"I've hung it at the door."

Pāka'a said, "Now only you can enter here because you've been made sacred for your haku by your handling of his kapa. From now on, you'll distribute the food in here to the 'ā'īpu'upu'u who come, because they can no longer enter."

Kūapāka'a went back out and noticed the ali'i was still without any kapa covering; compassion welled up in him, so he went and told his father, "Kā! my ali'i has a malo now, but no kapa. It's wrong for him to be without kapa to cover his skin."

Pāka'a took out the kapa he had once cared for and had stored in the wind gourd of La'amaomao when he left Hawai'i. He handed the kapa to his keiki and said, "Here's your haku's kapa. Give it to him. If he suspects it's his own, tell him your mother made it for you; through your crafty words, my presence will remain a secret."

As Kūapāka'a carried this kapa to the ali'i, he felt a strong desire to put it on himself because it was scented with aromatic leaves and other fragrances. The name of this kapa was 'Ō'ūholowai-o-La'a. Kūapāka'a said to the ali'i, "Here's my insignificant kapa for you to wear against the cold."

Keawenuia'umi grabbed it, looked it over closely, unfolded it, shook it out, smelled the fragrance, then asked the keiki, "Where did you find this kapa?"

The keiki answered, "On Moloka'i."

Keawenuia'umi said, "There's no kapa like this anywhere except on Hawai'i. It's not made for any other ali'i—only for me; so perhaps this is my kapa and perhaps Pāka'a is here on this island."

The keiki said, "My mother made this kapa for me because my mother, Hikauhi, and my father, Pālā'au, are ali'i. They looked for the very best kapa for me, one that was dyed and scented. Our fragrant kapa is called Wailau and the fragrant kapa of Hawai'i is called 'Ō'ūholowai-o-La'a. However, the fragrance is the same." This explanation quieted the ali'i's suspicions, and he put on the kapa without further questions.

When the aliʻi was dressed in the malo and kapa that Kūapākaʻa had brought him, everyone proceeded to the kauhale.

Keawenuiaʻumi had landed like a castaway and because the sea had robbed his kānaka of most of their supplies, they groped about clumsily to care for the needs of the aliʻi and themselves, no longer confident in themselves. On Hawaiʻi they were quick and well-prepared and won praise for their excellent work; but here on Molokaʻi, they had been humbled at sea and were timid. Had they followed the keiki's advice and landed in the first place, their reputations would have been saved; but because of their stubbornness, the aliʻi's malo and kapa had been soaked; the aliʻi would have had to remain on the canoe platform, if the keiki hadn't provided him with dry clothing.

Not only that, after the kauwā had been scolded by the aliʻi, they were listless, like drooping flowers, and sulky.

Before going to meet the fleet to urge Keawenuiaʻumi to come ashore, Pākaʻa and his keiki had prepared provisions for all the people who would travel with Keawenuiaʻumi.

When evening fell, Kūapākaʻa sent the six district aliʻi and their kānaka to the six hale he and his father had built. There were six hale for the six district aliʻi and their kānaka, and a separate hale for Keawenuiaʻumi. Each hale was full of kapa and other supplies the malihini needed.

At dinner time, Kūapākaʻa waited on Keawenuiaʻumi promptly, serving him carefully and neatly; and the aliʻi appreciated his expert care.

When night fell and everyone was at ease, Keawenuiaʻumi reminisced: "My love for Pākaʻa wells up in me. On evenings like this, my kauwā would bring me my cup of ʻawa and live hīnālea, and the intoxication would take effect; I would sit enjoying the intoxication of the ʻawa until I fell asleep; then I would sleep soundly all night long. How I miss Pākaʻa!"

Kūapākaʻa heard the words of the aliʻi and reported to his father: "Kā! My haku desires some ʻawa. He spoke of his love for you; when you were his kahu, you brought him his ʻawa. He misses it."

Pākaʻa took out an ʻawa preparation bowl and a cup, some grass for straining the ʻawa, a piece of dried ʻawa root, and portions of ʻawa root already chewed, which he tied into bundles. He put everything into a piece of trimmed kapa, which he took out of the wind gourd of Laʻamaomao, and told his keiki, "Take this dried ʻawa to your aliʻi and show it to him. If he tells you to chew it, look for a dark place and hide

68

the dried 'awa there, then strain this portion of already chewed 'awa into the bowl. He'll be impressed with how quickly you've prepared the 'awa for him. That's the way I did it when I was with him. After pouring the 'awa into the cup, serve the 'awa to him, then run quickly to the beach to get the live hīnālea we put into the small pond, and give them to your haku as pūpū to cut the bitterness of the 'awa."

Kūapāka'a took the 'awa and the other things to the ali'i and said, "Here's a little 'awa for you to drink."

When the ali'i saw the large dried 'awa root, he told the keiki, "You must chew my 'awa." The keiki turned away to a corner of the room and dropped the dried 'awa root there, then poured water into the preparation bowl and put into it the 'awa Pāka'a had already chewed. He strained the juice out of the chewed 'awa with the grass, then poured the juice into the cup and gave the cup to the ali'i. Then he ran to the beach and returned with two hīnālea wriggling about in his hands. He put them on a dish and placed the live hīnālea before the ali'i.

When Keawenuia'umi saw the tasty fish presented to him, he grabbed them gleefully, admiring the keiki for doing what an adult would have done; it was as if the keiki had lived with an ali'i because the keiki knew exactly what to do.

The ali'i was delighted with the 'awa and enjoyed his drinking; then, very tired from having almost drowned at sea, he fell asleep along with his kānaka.

After they were all asleep, Kūapāka'a opened his wind gourd, and the winds rushed out and a storm blew continuously for many days. The ali'i and his kānaka became very discouraged while waiting for good weather.

After the ali'i landed on Moloka'i and began living with Kūapāka'a, Pāka'a put into motion his plan to kill Ho'okele-i-Hilo and Ho'okele-i-Puna.

He told his keiki, "Let's go look for a hollow log."

"Why a log?"

"To store food inside."

"Why are we going to store food in a log?"

"The food will help us gain my revenge against my two enemies," said Pāka'a. They went and found a big, long log that was rotted hollow; they cleaned it out, then took it to the home of Ho'olehua mā, the parents of Hikauhi.

After they left the log there, Pāka'a told the keiki, "Let's go look for a big rock."

"Why a rock?"

"A rock anchor for the ali'i's canoe, to help us gain revenge against my two enemies."

They found a rock grooved in the middle so a rope could be tied securely around it.

When the log and the rock were ready, Pāka'a gave the keiki more instructions: "After the ali'i and his kānaka eat up all of their food, they'll come to you for more. That's when you'll give them the 'uala we planted in the uplands. Tell them not to throw away the small ones. They should prepare the small 'uala carefully—peel them, clean them, and set them out in the sun to dry. Then take the 'uala to the kauhale of your kūpuna and store them in the hollow log. Also put into the log some dried fish, some water gourds, the loulu fronds we brought down from the uplands, and finally, some coils of rope for the stone anchor.

"When your haku urges you to accompany him, refuse at first; then when he stubbornly insists, tell him that if your 'ope'ope can be put on board the canoe, you'll go with him. When he agrees, have the log and the rock loaded onto the canoe.

"When you sail beyond the sea of Ka'ie'iewaho to Kaua'i and turn at Waimea, open your wind gourd and let the winds blow and the rain and stormy weather pour out. Your haku will ask you what he should do. Tell him to drop the sea anchor. Unwind the coils of rope and tie one end around your stone anchor and the other to the canoe, then toss the anchor into the sea so the canoe won't be swept too far off course. If the kānaka are shivering from the rain and the cold, give out the loulu fronds for protection to everyone except Ho'okele-i-Hilo and Ho'okele-i-Puna. If you see that the kānaka are hungry and thirsty, give the dried sweet potatoes, fish, and water to everyone, except Ho'okele-i-Hilo and Ho'okele-i-Puna. Eventually the two of them will die from the cold. After my revenge is complete, cover the gourd and sail with your haku to Hawai'i. Then return to me here."

All these commands were carried out faithfully by the keiki.

He went and filled the log with food; the stormy months ended and the days of good weather returned.

Keawenuia'umi, the district ali'i, and the kānaka remained on Moloka'i waiting for good weather. After the month of Welehu passed, the little food that was left after the canoes had been swamped at sea was gone, so one of the district aliʻi sent his ʻelele to Keawenuiaʻumi. When the ʻelele came before the aliʻi, the aliʻi asked him, "What brings you here?"

The ʻelele replied, "I've been sent by my aliʻi to tell you we've eaten all that was left after our canoes were swamped at sea, so we've come to ask you what we should do."

Keawenuiaʻumi said, "One of you should go to the keiki—perhaps he has some food."

One of the kānaka went to Kūapākaʻa and said, "The aliʻi has sent for you."

The two of them went before Keawenuiaʻumi, and the aliʻi said to Kūapākaʻa, "I've summoned you because our food is gone and my people are starving. If you have any food left over, give it to them."

Kūapākaʻa replied, "ʻAe, I have a little food in the uplands. For the six district aliʻi, there are six little patches of ʻuala and six little clumps of kō. Here's what you should do to make sure there's enough food. When you go and gather the food, don't leave the small tubers and stalks behind. If you gather everything, you'll have enough to eat and won't have to gather more."

"You have only six little patches of ʻuala and six little clumps of kō, ē ke keiki? How will all these kānaka be fed?"

"The ʻuala here bears tubers only when it sees the kānaka themselves are productive. The same with the kō—only when it sees the kānaka increasing in number does the kō grow lushly."

Here's the reason for the keiki's words: he knew some of the aliʻi's kānaka were lazy, especially his hangers-on, so when he said that only when the ʻuala sees the kānaka, the plants bear tubers, he meant that only when the kānaka went to dig the ʻuala from the mounds would there be an abundance of food; so too with the kō: the cuttings without flowers had been planted, so the kō had grown wild and bushy. But the lazy ones wouldn't see the lush growth unless they went to harvest the kō in the uplands.

Keawenuiaʻumi and the six district aliʻi and their kānaka just laughed at the keiki's answer; thus, some went to the uplands, while some stayed back.

Kūapākaʻa accompanied the six district aliʻi and their kānaka to the uplands and pointed out the ʻuala and the kō. When the aliʻi and their kānaka saw the abundance of food—so much 'uala and kō, their eyes would go blind before seeing it all—they said to themselves: "Kā! The keiki said only six little patches of 'uala and six little clumps of kō, but here are many long rows of 'uala and many fields of kō growing tall and lush."

The eyes would go blind before seeing all of the 'uala, and the kānaka could lay down and disappear in the fields of kō.

When the kānaka saw the great abundance of 'ai and kō, they returned to the coast and got those who had stayed back. They all dug the 'ai and pulled up the kō, doing just as the keiki had told them to do, taking even the small 'uala, so they wouldn't have to return for more later. The district ali'i and all their kānaka were exhausted before all the fields of 'uala were harvested.

When the ali'i and their kānaka finally returned to the seacoast with the 'uala and kō and lit their imu, Kūapāka'a told them, "The big 'uala are yours, the small ones are mine."

"Kāhāhā!" they said. "That's not so—all of them, big and small, are yours."

"'A'ole, the big 'uala are yours, the small ones are mine. When you finish peeling the small ones, lay them out in the sun to dry."

They asked, "Why should we do that?"

"I've asked you to harvest my 'uala fields because the months when the seas are stormy are upon us and your stay here will be long. Welehu will pass and three months of bad weather will follow—Makali'i, Kā'elo and Kaulua.[50] When Nana comes, perhaps there will be good weather again, and that's when you'll be able to leave. While you're here you'll consume all of my food. I won't starve or be deprived of food because I'll have the small 'uala to eat while I plant food crops again."

The kānaka took care of the small 'uala, according to the keiki's advice to be thrifty—every time they baked any 'ai, they dried the small ones in the sun and took them to Kūapāka'a.

Kūapāka'a's words hid his real purpose. He had served the ali'i so skillfully, he knew Keawenuia'umi liked him and would urge him to come along with them to look for Pāka'a. Kūapāka'a had the dried 'uala prepared so he could take it with him for food on the voyage, as his father had instructed him to do.

After the kānaka had gathered their 'ai, they went down to the beach, kicked up the water, and stranded baby mullet on the sand; thus, they obtained some iʻa to go along with their ʻai; they ate the famous fish of this place, that is, "the fish kicked ashore at Hīlia."[51] That's how they subsisted during their three-month wait for good weather.

Before Keawenuiaʻumi mā sailed from Hawaiʻi, they had told the makaʻāinana they would be gone a month, but more than three months had passed, so the people of Hawaiʻi thought the aliʻi had died at sea, and everyone grieved for him—the men, women, and children, the overseeers of ahupuaʻa and the makaʻāinana. But while they grieved, their aliʻi was alive on Molokaʻi, detained there by Kūapākaʻa.

Keawenuiaʻumi and his district aliʻi and their kānaka lived on Molokaʻi for four months. They missed dearly the people of Hawaiʻi they had left behind and longed for their wives and children; their thoughts were sad.

When Kūapākaʻa knew that the stormy months he had spoken of had passed, he covered his wind gourd and calm seas returned. He told the aliʻi, "This is the month of Nana, when good weather returns; Welo and Ikiiki will follow, months when the fishermen's lines are always wet because the seas are calm, and the fisherman goes out often."[52]

Kūapākaʻa urged the district aliʻi and their kānaka to secure the lashings and riggings of the canoes and prepare to sail because the weather was good: "I've asked you to remain here during the stormy months, but now the seas are calm again, and it's all right for you to leave. Secure the lashings and riggings of the canoes and anchor the canoes offshore, then go to sleep and rest your eyes, for the aliʻi's journey is about to begin again, and you must prepare yourselves to go."

The district aliʻi commanded their kānaka to secure the lashings and riggings of the canoes, and when all was secure, the canoes were paddled out through the channel, and anchored offshore. Late that evening, everyone went to sleep; but before long, Kūapākaʻa got up and called out to the district aliʻi and their kānaka to get up and leave in their canoes, even though it wasn't dawn, which was the customary time for aliʻi to depart in the old days. Kīauau[53] usually roused the aliʻi for departure, but Kūapākaʻa was up before him and called out in a loud voice:

Get up! Get up!! Get up!!!
It's near midnight, it's near daylight,
Gone are the tiredness, the soreness, the lameness,
The faintness of the crew,

73

Get up, get up, there above,
Hikili'imakaounulau,
The morning star is at the border of the land,
Get up, move, let's go.

When the ali'i mā heard the keiki calling, they mistakenly thought it was Kīauau, so they said to each other, "Strange that Kīauau should awaken us to go at night."
One said, "Wait! Kīauau has never done this before, but perhaps he's anxious to go—he was unhappy that we had to stay here so long."
Because the kānaka didn't get up, Kūapāka'a called out again:

Get up! Get up!! Get up!!!
It's near midnight, it's near daylight,
Gone are the tiredness, the soreness, the lameness,
The faintness of the crew,
Get up, get up, there above,
Hikili'imakaounulau,
The morning star is at the border of the land,
Get up, move, let's go.

Some of the kānaka got up at the keiki's calling, but the ali'i and the others remained asleep. The kānaka who got up went outside and saw it wasn't Kīauau, but Kūapāka'a, who had roused them, and they were very annoyed that their pleasant sleep had been disturbed: "Kā! The keiki is strange! It's not even dawn and he's calling us to get up. It's still in the middle of the night, yet the keiki's telling us to get up because Hikili'imakaounulau is above." (In ancient times the people of Hawai'i called the last star appearing at dawn Hikili'imakao-unulau.)[54]
The district ali'i had heard the second calling, but they and the other kānaka wanted to sleep some more and give their eyes a rest; only when Ka I'a turned in the sky after midnight would they get up and prepare to go. Kūapāka'a waited in the dark, and when the ali'i didn't get up, he decided to call the names of the six districts of Hawai'i to drive the ali'i out of their hale:

Get up, Kona, land of the sea soothed
    by the Kēhau breeze,
The shady clouds of Ke'ei are flying,

74

The clouds are like roof-thatching
    above the breadfruit groves of Weli,
How long you've slept, even though I call you,
You rest calmly and do not stir.
Get up, Kohala,
Move, Kohala, all together,
Papa stirs, the one who gave birth
    to the islands of Ko'olau.
Get up, Hilo,
Hilo, with its adze-headed rain brought
    by the Unulau wind,
    the hair straight on the pandanus pillow,
The lehua blossoms open in the zigzagging rain,
In the calm, the kī-leaves are braided
    onto the edge of the net,
To catch the nehu in the sea of Punahoa.
Get up, Puna,
Puna, land fragrant with hala,
From the heights to the seashore grass,
The red of Kailua,
A-ē 'ae kukio, the wind of Ka'ū,
Get up, Ka'ū,
Ka'ū, the vast, windy land,
Ko'a, the current to Hala'ea,
Where the canoes hurry to leave,
To leave for Kā'iliki'i, for Kaulana,
The canoes for one go, the canoes for two go,
The canoes for three go, the canoes for four go,
The canoes for five go, the canoes for six go,
The canoes for seven go, the canoes for eight go,
The canoes for nine go, the canoes for ten go,
The baggage canoes go, the small canoes,
The red-sailed canoes of the ali'i go.

When the district ali'i heard the keiki calling, they knew he was
calling them; they woke up grumbling about having to get up and
prepare to sail when they hadn't slept enough. They didn't go outside at
first, but sat at the edge of their mats and listened as Kūapāka'a called
again.

A little while after he had called the names of the lands, Kūapāka'a called out again because he thought the ali'i were still not up. In this calling, he named not just the six lands, but the six ali'i who ruled these lands because he was sure that when they heard their names, they would get up and prepare to go. First he called those of Kohala:

Get up, get up, it's day, there's light,
The sun has arrived, and there above,
Iao [the planet Jupiter], Maiao [a navigation star],
Kamaha, Kahikikuokamoku,
Kani-'ū'ū, the star at Helani,
Get up, move, Kohala,
The land of Wahilani.

When Wahilani and his kānaka heard Kūapāka'a's call, they all got up and prepared to go, but when Wahilani saw Kūapāka'a was the one calling, he grumbled, "It's not this keiki's duty to drive us from our hale."

When Kūapāka'a saw that Wahilani and his kānaka were awake, he called those of Hāmākua:

Get up, get up, it's day, there's light,
The keiki of the wind urges you,
The daughter of the wind of Malanai,
Of Malanai, of Ku, of Ha'eha'e,
The sail crackles in the wind,
Kaulua, Hinaia'ele'ele,
The stormy months of the islands,
Get up, get up, Hāmākua,
The land of Wanu'a.

When Wanu'a heard Kūapāka'a's calling, he said to his kānaka, "Let's get up, don't sleep anymore." They all got up and prepared to go, but when Wanu'a saw Kūapāka'a was the caller, he said, "Kā! How puzzling!—I thought it was Kīauau waking us up while it's still evening, but it's the keiki. It's not this keiki's duty to drive us from our hale."

After the ali'i of Hāmākua and his kānaka were awake, Kūapāka'a called those of Hilo:

Get up, get up, it's day, there's light,
The keiki who nets the schools of nehu urges you,
The rain draws the schools of nehu seaward of Punahoa,
The adze-headed rain in the Unulau wind,
The lehua blossoms open in the zigzagging rain,
The warm rain of the land of Hilo,
Get up, get up, Hilo,
The land of Kulukulu'ā.

Kulukulu'ā heard his land being called, so he got up and awakened his kānaka saying, "Those of you still asleep, get up and prepare to go. Here's the call." They all got up and prepared to go, but when Kulukulu'ā saw Kūapāka'a was the caller, he grumbled, "Our eyes are open, and we're awake; but it's not this keiki's duty to drive us from our hale."

When Kūapāka'a saw Hilo's ali'i and kānaka were awake, he called those of Puna.

Get up, get up, it's day, there's light,
The sun emerges at Kumukahi,
Shining like Makanoni,
Puna whose bowers are fragrant with hala,
From the heights of Akoakoa,
Puna is a proud land for her people,
Get up, get up, Puna,
The land of Hua'ā.

Hua'ā heard his land being called and awakened all his kānaka, saying, "Get up, don't turn again in the kapa covers, here's the call."

Those of Puna woke up and prepared to depart, but when Hua'ā saw Kūapāka'a was the caller, he grumbled, "Kā! Here it's still evening and we're being awakened. The keiki is strange. It's not this keiki's duty to drive us from our hale."

He said angrily, "You're wahahe'e, ē ke keiki. Who says the lā (sun) emerges at Kumukahi when it's still evening?"

Kūapāka'a said, "Lā does appear. The native son waits at the cape of Kumukahi and when the sun sets, he lies down for a while but doesn't sleep. He gets up when the 'ōpelu runs, and goes down to the seashore, boards his canoe, hoists his lā (sail), and sets off. Thus, lā does appear at

Kumukahi when it's still evening."⁵⁵

"You're right, ē ke keiki," said the gathering of kānaka. "Huaʻā is forced to rise because lā appears in his land both night and day."

Kūapākaʻa saw the aliʻi and the kānaka of Puna were awake, so he called the people of Kaʻū.

Get up, get up, it's day, there's light,
Get up, Kaʻū, windy land,
ʻAe-ʻae kukio, wind of Kaʻū,
Koʻa, the current at Halaʻea,
The canoes hurry to leave,
For Kāʻilikiʻi, for Ka Lae,
For Kaulanamauna,
Get up, get up, Kaʻū,
The land of Mākaha.

Mākaha heard his land being called and was embarrassed, so he told his kānaka, "Get up. You heard the call, yet nobody's up. Our compound is cursed by a loud voice." Everyone from Kaʻū got up and prepared to leave.

Some kānaka told Mākaha, "That's Kūapākaʻa awakening us." Mākaha turned to the keiki and said, "My land is famous as a windy land, but its wind doesn't blow kānaka around, only rubbish. Molokaʻi's wind is this puffing little keiki who blows away anyone who doesn't hold on tight in his hale. Yet it's not this keiki's duty to drive us from our hale."

Kūapākaʻa answered, "Your land's wind is perhaps famous, but it's not a real wind for it carries only empty words. No other land is as windy as Molokaʻi. You don't know:

Hoʻolua-iho at Hālawa,
Hoʻolua-noe at Hālawa,
Hoʻolua-kele at Hālawa,
Hoʻolua-pelu at Hālawa,
Hoʻolua-kaipou at Hālawa,
Hoʻolua-wahakole at Hālawa,
Hikipua at Hālawa,
Aano at Hālawa,
Lau-kamani at Hālawa,
Puuohoku at Hālawa,

Okia at Hālawa,
Ualehua at Hālawa,
Laiku at Hālawa,
Naulu at Hālawa,
Kehau at Hālawa,
Koi-pali at Hālawa,
Lī-anu at Hālawa,
Ehukai at Hālawa.

"It's frightening when all these winds blow together strongly. No one stays in the hale because these winds blow down hale and blow away anyone who doesn't hold on tightly inside the hale."

"You're right, ē ke keiki," said the gathering of kānaka. "Blow Mākaha and us back to his windy land."

After those of Ka'ū were awake, Kūapāka'a called those of Kona:

Get up, get up, it's day, there's light,
The hands are washed, the food is eaten,
Koena-ulu, Koena-kihapai are of Ka'awaloa,
Aku-aku is of Maka'ula,
Ahi-aku is of Awalua,
The night rises, rises until full,
Here's the sea at the 'ākulikuli,
At the pohuehue
Growing on the beach,
Kona, get up, Kona,
Kona, land soothed by the Kēhau breeze,
The shady clouds of Ke'ei are flying above,
The clouds are like roof-thatching
    above the groves of Leiwalu,
Get up, get up, Kona,
The land of 'Ehu.

'Ehu refused to get up when he heard the other ali'i being called, but when he heard the call for his land, he said to his kānaka, "Kona, wake up, you're being called, open your eyes and get up." Everyone from Kona got up and prepared to depart. When 'Ehu saw Kūapāka'a was the caller, 'Ehu grumbled, "Ka I'a hasn't turned yet, but you're rousing us from sleep. It's not this keiki's duty to drive us from our hale."

Earlier, as the district ali'i were preparing their canoes for the voyage, an 'elele of the ali'i had told the district ali'i to go first and wait offshore, and Keawenuia'umi would follow later. So the district ali'i and their kānaka, prodded by the keiki, boarded their canoes and left; only the ali'i's canoe remained on Moloka'i.

The canoes headed for Ka'ula to look for Pāka'a as Keawenuia'umi had told them to; but since Keawenuia'umi had also ordered them to heave to and wait for his canoe, as they were passing outside of Lē'ahi, O'ahu, they turned around.

While they were heading back, all the ali'i and the kānaka were still very tired because Kūapāka'a had awakened them so early in the evening; they fell asleep; only the ho'okele remained awake. They tried to stay up until dawn, but because they, too, were very tired, and the rest of the kānaka were snoring, they lowered the sails and fell asleep.

When the ho'okele awoke, they thought they were still in the Moloka'i Channel. They raised their sails and set off again heading east back to Moloka'i. Then the district ali'i and their kānaka also woke up. At dawn they saw some faint mountain ridges and thought these were the Maui mountains, but when daylight came, they knew they were off the island of Hawai'i, so they entered the channel and landed at Kawaihae. The district ali'i and the kānaka were happy to see their island again and eager to see their wives, children, parents, and the rest of their 'ohana.

When they landed, there was great excitement among the men, women, and children on shore because those who had gone in search of Pāka'a were thought to be dead but here they had returned alive. The maka'āinana of Keawenuia'umi were still grieving, but when they heard the ali'i and his kānaka were alive on Moloka'i, they ended their mourning and rejoiced along with the others.

After the district ali'i and their kānaka had sailed away, Kūapāka'a went back to sleep without awakening Keawenuia'umi. Near dawn the keiki got up, went outside, and called loudly:

Get up, get up, you, Kilaupale,
O'ahu's water, above O'ahu's mountains,
Kaunuohua, tall and majestic,
The darting hills of Nihoa,
This cliff, that cliff,

Pālā'au, Kahiwa-iluna,
Get up, get up, great Hawai'i of Kāne.

When the hoewa'a of the ali'i heard the keiki's call, they all woke up and prepared to depart.

Keawenuia'umi had slept soundly that night. When morning came and he heard the keiki's calling, he woke up and sent a kahu to summon Kūapāka'a. The kahu found the keiki and told him, "I've come to get you; the ali'i commands you to go to him."

"'Ae, let's go," replied Kūapāka'a.

When the keiki arrived before Keawenuia'umi, the ali'i told the keiki, "Let's you and I sail together to Ka'ula to look for Pāka'a."

"I can't. I have to stay here and take care of some problems with my small hut. No one will take care of it if I go."

The ali'i urged him to go: "Sail with me. We won't be gone long, we'll come back shortly."

"I can't. I've just told you why I can't."

The ali'i persisted: "Don't worry about your little hut; we'll return shortly."

The ali'i stubbornly insisted that the keiki go with him, so Kūapāka'a finally said, "Ē my haku, I'll sail with you if you'll agree to load my little 'ope'ope on your canoe. Otherwise, I won't go with you."

"'Ae, let's sail together. Some kānaka will be sent for your 'ope'ope."

The ali'i ordered some of his kānaka to go with the keiki to get the keiki's 'ope'ope. When they arrived at the place where Ho'olehua lived, they found outside the clearing a big log as long as the ali'i's canoe. The keiki said to the kānaka, "Here's my little 'ope'ope. You two, load it onto the ali'i's canoe, then come back."

"Kā! You're the greatest liar who's ever lived. You said you had a little 'ope'ope, but you have a big log. It's much too big for the canoe!"

Grumbling, the kānaka lifted the log and carried it down to the ali'i's canoe. When the hoewa'a and ho'okele of Keawenuia'umi's canoe saw the log, they asked the kānaka, "What's this log for?"

"It's the keiki's 'ope'ope—the ali'i agreed to load it onto the canoe. If he had seen the size of the keiki's 'ope'ope, he would have refused."

After the log was carried onto the canoe, the kānaka returned to get Kūapāka'a. The keiki pointed to a big rock with a piece of cord tied about its grooved middle; he told the kānaka, "Here's another little 'ope'ope.

You two, load it onto the ali'i's canoe."

"You're really strange, ē ke keiki. I've served the ali'i a long time and my hair is gray, but I've never seen anyone sail with a rock for 'ope'ope. You're the only one."

Kūapāka'a said, "Women have sailed with you."

"What about women? We're talking about a rock," said the kānaka.

"A rock is like a woman," said Kūapāka'a. "When our ali'i go to Maui and want a woman to accompany them, the hoewa'a protest, 'A woman is a rock, a burden on the canoe.'"

"You're right again, ē ke keiki, and we're wrong. The ali'i has indeed sailed with a rock because women have sailed with him before."

Grumbling, the kānaka lifted the rock and carried it down to the ali'i's canoe. When the hoewa'a and the ho'okele saw it, they asked the kānaka, "What's this rock doing here?"

"It's the keiki's 'ope'ope, which the ali'i agreed to load onto the canoe—if he had seen the size of the keiki's 'ope'ope, he would have refused."

Someone else criticized the keiki indirectly by saying, "The children of Kaluako'i carry really big 'ope'ope with them."

The kānaka said, "It's huge, but bring it aboard the canoe anyway."

After the kānaka loaded the rock onto the canoe, they waited for the ali'i. Meanwhile Kūapāka'a went into the hale 'āipu'upu'u and told his father, "My ukana are on board the canoe."

"'Ae, that's good," said Pāka'a. "Go—go and remember the words of your father."

"'Ae," said Kūapāka'a. "I go in your place to do your work. I may die, but what of it?—it's done. If I'm not killed, I'll kill your enemies and you'll be avenged."

Kūapāka'a took his wind gourd and went outside. He went to the place where the ali'i was living and said, "My little 'ope'ope are on board the canoe. Come, let's go."

The ali'i, his kānaka, and Kūapāka'a went down to where the double-hulled canoe was anchored and boarded it. Kūapāka'a sat in front of the kānaka who were seated in front of the ho'okele, and when everyone was seated in his proper place, the canoe departed. When the hoewa'a saw Kūapāka'a with the ali'i, they remarked, "Here's the keiki from Kaluako'i with the big 'ope'ope." From then on, this saying has been used to refer to anyone traveling with bulky baggage.

The sail was hoisted and the native wind from Kona, a Moaʻe, blew; the two hoʻokele held the steering paddles at the stern of the canoe. As Kūapākaʻa watched the hoʻokele and admired their work, he felt a desire to have one of the steering paddles entrusted to him so he could experience the joy of being a hoʻokele. He told the hoʻokele: "Give me one of your paddles—I'll hold it tightly while I enjoy steering the canoe with you two."

The hoʻokele replied, "We can't let you hold one of our paddles. Don't you know it's our duty to steer. It would be wrong for us to entrust one of the paddles to you."

After being rebuffed, Kūapākaʻa stopped asking. The keiki was testing the two hoʻokele—if the hoʻokele had allowed him to hold one of the paddles, perhaps they might have escaped death.

The canoe went past Oʻahu and across the sea of Kaʻieʻiewaho to Kauaʻi, then past Kōloa. When it was directly off Waimea, Kūapākaʻa uncovered of the wind gourd of Laʻamaomao, and a big storm overtook the canoe.

The winds blew hard, driving the canoe out into the open sea. The skies darkened, lightning flashed, thunder roared, and rain pelted down. The storm was boundless. The canoe was buffeted by the wind, and Kauaʻi almost disappeared. The kānaka shivered from the cold rain and waves breaking over the canoe from the front, the back, and the sides.

But the aliʻi wasn't worried about the storm because he had great confidence in the keiki. This was why he had begged the keiki to come with him. When Keawenuiaʻumi saw that the island had almost disappeared, he asked his hoʻokele, "What should we do? The storm is getting worse."

They didn't answer because the waves were swamping the canoe, and they were concentrating their efforts on bailing the canoe to prevent it from sinking.

Since the hoʻokele didn't answer, Keawenuiaʻumi decided the time was right to ask the keiki what to do. The aliʻi remembered the keiki had advised him wisely about the first storm, so he trusted that the keiki would give him good advice now: "Say, you there, what should we do? What a storm! We're getting chilled to the bone by the cold rain and sea water."

Kūapākaʻa responded, "I don't have anything to offer, except perhaps my little rock—we could lower it into the sea to prevent the canoe from drifting. It's better for us to stay in one place than to get blown by the wind out of sight of land. When the storm stops, we can return to land."

Then Kūapāka'a opened one end of his big log, thrust in his hand, and pulled out a rope. After he tied one end of the rope firmly to the grooved rock and the other end to the canoe, the hoewa'a threw the rock overboard. With the canoe dragging this sea anchor, they waited for the storm to pass. When the keiki had opened the end of his log to take out the rope, the kānaka saw for the first time the log was hollow and filled with provisions.[56]

Kūapāka'a saw the ali'i and the kānaka suffering from the cold, extremely bedraggled, their bodies shivering in the chilly air and cramping in the rain. The keiki thrust his hand into the log again and pulled out the loulu palm leaves he and his father had gathered; he passed them out to the ali'i and the kānaka, but not to Ho'okele-i-Hilo and Ho'okele-i-Puna; so everybody had protection from the rain except the two ho'okele.

When Kūapāka'a saw the kānaka slapping their bodies to keep themselves limber, he took some 'ai and i'a out of the log and fed the ali'i and the kānaka, but again he left out Ho'okele-i-Hilo and Ho'okele-i-Puna. The ali'i and his kānaka felt warmer after eating the food, while the ho'okele continued to shiver because they didn't get any.

After the kānaka had eaten their fill, Kūapāka'a took the water gourds out of the log and let all the kānaka drink—except Ho'okele-i-Hilo and Ho'okele-i-Puna.

When the two ho'okele weren't given loulu palm leaves to protect themselves, they knew they would succumb to the cold. They suffered patiently. The keiki didn't answer them when they asked him for some protection and for some 'ai, i'a, and wai. Then they recalled the keiki's words, "You two will become fearful and weak on board the canoe, then fall overboard into the sea." They realized that soon this prophecy would be fulfilled.

Kūapāka'a saw the ho'okele waiting patiently in the cold, slapping and pounding themselves to keep their bodies limber. Their bodies were stiffening and going into shock, and their skin was turning blue. Their bodies were chilled by the cold and numbed by the rain above, the sea below, and the wind coming at them from all sides. The keiki knew Ho'okele-i-Hilo and Ho'okele-i-Puna would die, and he felt sorry for them, but he had to obey his father's orders. He suppressed his compassion for his fellow human beings so he could carry out his father's revenge.

Before long the kānaka heard the sound of a body falling into the sea behind the canoe, and when the hoewaʻa who sat in front of Hoʻokele-i-Hilo looked behind, he didn't see the hoʻokele, so he announced, "Hoʻokele-i-Hilo is dead; he has fallen into the sea."

"Auwē, aloha ʻino," said the kānaka.

Not long after, they heard the sound of another body falling into the sea, and the hoewaʻa who sat in front of Hoʻokele-i-Puna glanced behind and saw the hoʻokele wasn't there, so he announced, "Hoʻokele-i-Puna is dead; he has fallen into the sea."

"Auwē, aloha ʻino," said the kānaka.

Thus, Hoʻokele-i-Hilo and Hoʻokele-i-Puna died at sea. They had pursued Pākaʻa in the sea of ʻAlenuihāhā in order to destroy him; instead, they were destroyed by Pākaʻa's keiki. The evil they had intended toward Pākaʻa had turned back on them.

When Kūapākaʻa saw his father's enemies had drowned, he covered the wind gourd and the storm quickly subsided, and the sea became calm.

Keawenuiaʻumi asked the keiki, "What now? My hoʻokele are dead and I don't have any other hoʻokele on board. Will you guide the canoe for us?"

"Why not? Perhaps I'll try," the keiki replied.

Kūapākaʻa went to the stern of the canoe where the hoʻokele stood and became the aliʻi's hoʻokele-waʻa. Keawenuiaʻumi conferred the duties of guiding the canoe on Kūapākaʻa; everyone's life or death was in the keiki's hands.

Keawenuiaʻumi told the keiki, "Since the weather's good, let's go to Kaʻula to look for my kahu Pākaʻa."

Kūapākaʻa agreed and turned the canoe toward Kaʻula.

When the sun came out and warmed the canoe, the aliʻi and the kānaka grew drowsy and fell asleep. As soon as Kūapākaʻa saw everyone was asleep, he turned the canoe back toward Oʻahu. Then he opened the wind gourd of Laʻamaomao, and fair winds blew from behind the canoe. In no time they passed the leeward coast of Oʻahu, after which Kūapākaʻa pointed the canoe toward the cliffs of Kaholo and from there around the southern coast of Kahoʻolawe. By nightfall, the canoe was in the sea of ʻAlenuihāhā. When the kānaka awoke, it was night and the wind was blowing from behind them; they thought the canoe was heading toward Kaʻula.

At dawn they saw mountains and some kānaka realized they had returned to Hawaiʻi. Others disagreed, but as the canoe approached shore, everyone knew for sure they were off the coast of Hawaiʻi, and everyone rejoiced; only Keawenuiaʻumi was sad because he regretted he hadn't found Pākaʻa.

When the canoe was close to the shore at Kawaihae, the kānaka wanted to land quickly so they could see their wives, children, and close friends. Kūapākaʻa saw the excitement of the kānaka and asked indirectly about his fate, "Ē, how many of you will remember the keiki?"

"Why do you wonder?" asked one kanaka.

"He'll be neglected after the canoe is carried ashore," said the keiki.

"Why will you be neglected?" Lapakahoe asked.

Kūapākaʻa replied, "I see that you're all eager to land quickly. When we land, all of you will jump off the canoe and kiss your wives and rub noses with your children. You'll weep over your wives and children and embrace them; you'll greet your parents, grandparents, and close friends. You'll call out the names of your children and grieve for the children who have become orphans. While all of you are busy with this and that, I'll be forgotten—a friendless person here."

"You won't be neglected by the aliʻi," said Lapakahoe, "because you saved all of us in the storm."

"Perhaps that's so," said Kūapākaʻa, "but I believe the keiki will be forgotten once the canoe is carried ashore."

These words of Kūapākaʻa turned out to be true because when the canoe landed, the aliʻi and all the kānaka jumped off quickly and left him behind. The aliʻi and his kahu, koa, and kānaka were quickly surrounded by their wives, children, parents, grandparents, and close friends, all of whom wept for joy. The people called out the names Keawenuiaʻumi and Kahikuokamoku to welcome them. Those who had stayed behind and those who had sailed mixed together, and excitement, frenzy, and confusion spread through the crowd. Everyone was overjoyed because the aliʻi had returned alive. The friends with whom Kūapākaʻa had sailed scattered here and there, and the keiki was indeed forgotten.

When the greetings and the shouts of joy at the beach subsided, the people returned to their hale. The keiki waited to be called, but no one invited him home. He was truly neglected.

After returning to their kauhale, the people prepared their imu to cook puaʻa and moa. When they dug open their imu, they sat down to feast.

Still, no one thought to invite the keiki to eat.

The keiki sniffed the aroma of the cooking, and his mouth watered as he thought about the delicious food. He said to himself, "I'm hungry for pua'a; but I said I'd be forgotten once the canoe was carried ashore, and I've been forgotten."

He waited to be invited to a feast when everyone else had eaten, but even then, he wasn't invited anywhere. No one remembered him, not even the ali'i.

Here's the reason the keiki was neglected: the kānaka all assumed the ali'i would remember the keiki because they wouldn't have gotten back to land or escaped death at sea if it hadn't been for the keiki. Not only that, the ali'i had appointed the keiki as his ho'okele, so the kānaka assumed the ali'i had taken the keiki to the aloali'i with him; but of course he hadn't.

The ali'i, on his part, had supposed the kānaka would remember the keiki because without the keiki they would never have seen Hawai'i again.

The ali'i also believed that since the keiki had fed the kānaka with 'ai and i'a when they were confined by stormy weather on Moloka'i, the crew would remember the keiki's generosity; but they didn't.

Thus, the keiki's prediction that he would be neglected came true.

In the evening Kūapāka'a realized everyone had forgotten him, so he tidied up and cleaned the ali'i's canoe, and stayed there. The canoe became his shelter, and he lived there day and night. He had provisions, since there was still a lot of dried fish, dried sweet potato and water left in his log. Eating dried fish and dried sweet potato was better than starving. Thus, he was able to live without friends in Kawaihae until mālolo season arrived.

One evening Kūapāka'a heard a luna kāhea announce that at dawn canoes would go mālolo fishing. The keiki was hungry for fresh fish.

At dawn Kūapāka'a got up and strolled down the beach to where the fishermen kept their canoes. He met two of them securing the lashings of their canoe.

"Are you going for mālolo?" the keiki asked.

"'Ae, what's it to you?"

"May I go along with you two?"

"'A'ole," said one of the kānaka. "Only the two of us are going in our canoe."

"A canoe has to have a bailer," said Kūapāka'a. "If I go with you, you won't have to give me any of your share of the catch. I know how this kind of fishing is carried out: if the catch is large, all of us pāhoe will get our shares by ka'au, or forties; if the catch is small, then our shares will be by kāuna, or fours; in either case, I won't get any of your shares."

Kūapāka'a was right, so one of the kānaka said, "'Ae, come with us then."

Kūapāka'a helped secure the canoe's lashings and carry it into the water; then the three of them boarded the canoe and set out with the rest of the fishing fleet. The fleet gathered mālolo from dawn until the sun lost its red glow. The catch was big, so the fish was divided by ka'au among all the pāhoe. After the fishermen and their paddlers got their shares of fish as well, the canoes began returning one by one to the channel to shore.

As Kūapāka'a mā leisurely paddled their canoe back to shore, he saw a big canoe with six kānaka in it; as he watched them paddling, he suddenly felt like racing with them, so he asked his two companions, "Shall we race against that canoe? Let's bet our ka'au of mālolo against their ka'au."

"Kā-hā-hā! How can we beat those kānaka? It would be six of them against three of us," said one of the companions.

"You should get into that canoe, so it would be seven of you against two of us," replied Kūapāka'a.

"Kā-hā-hā! I won't be your partner either, ē kēnā keiki," said the other kanaka. "I don't want to lose my ka'au of mālolo. You aren't strong enough to paddle against those grown men."

"Then both of you should get into that canoe, so it'll be eight of you against me alone. We'll race, your ka'au of mālolo against mine. If the eight of you get to shore first, my fish will be yours; if I get to shore first, yours will be mine."

"All right," said the two kānaka. "We'll call that canoe over and if they agree, we'll race."

They called to the canoe with the six kānaka, and when the two canoes came together, the two kānaka told the six in the other canoe, "This keiki is strange. He wants to race—all of us in your canoe against him alone in this canoe, our ka'au of mālolo against his ka'au."

"What? Race to see how strong a paddler that feisty keiki is?"

They quickly accepted the keiki's challenge to race because they outnumbered him, and they believed they could easily win his ka'au of mālolo for themselves.

Kūapākaʻa anticipated losing a race against the six-man canoe if his two companions accepted his dare to join its crew, because their canoe was small and swift whereas the canoe he was in was big and heavy. When one of his partners declined to race against the six kānaka for fear of being defeated, and the other partner declined because he didn't want to lose his kaʻau of fish, Kūapākaʻa knew he couldn't win against those kānaka, but in keeping with his hard-headed and aggressive nature as a child, he goaded his two companions to join the other crew.

Kūapākaʻa's mocking behavior was meant to show those adults he wasn't ashamed to challenge all of them by himself; not that they paid any attention—all they were thinking about was winning the keiki's kaʻau of fish so they could get more fish to take to their kauhale.

After the race was agreed upon, and Kūapākaʻa's companions boarded the other canoe, the kānaka said, "Ē ke keiki, load your fish into our canoe."

"ʻAʻole," said Kūapākaʻa. "It's fairer if you load your fish into my canoe because if we race and I beat you, you might refuse to give up your fish; so even if I try my best and win, you might beat me up and not give me the fish. All the fish ought to be loaded into my canoe. If you win the race, I won't be able to keep the fish from you because there are too many of you. So why are you afraid of me?"

What Kūapākaʻa said was true, so they transfered all the fish to his canoe.

While they were transfering the fish, one of the kānaka commented, "This is a bother—why should we wait till we get to shore to take your fish when we know the greater number of paddlers will win the race?"

The keiki replied, "Perhaps. But the old folks of our place used to say, 'The big hau tree has a groove worn into it by a little hau tree.'"[57]

The kānaka were annoyed by the keiki's boastful words: "This keiki is really insolent!"

"The saying isn't mine," said Kūapākaʻa. "It's an ancient proverb."

As the two canoes paddled together, Kūapākaʻa admired the skill of the kānaka as they stroked evenly on one side, then the other, driving the canoe straight ahead.

When he saw he was in position to begin the race with them, he called out, "Listen, let's start from here!"

"ʻAe," they said.

When the two canoes were at a standstill and lined up, one of the kānaka called out, "Go! Paddle!"

The canoes started forward together, but soon Kūapāka'a was very far behind, and he saw he was going to be beaten by the eight men, so he said to himself, "Paddle all you like; if you beat me, I'll overturn this canoe in the lagoon, so all the fish will spill into the sea and no one will have any."

As he paddled along slowly, the keiki remembered hearing the story of how his father, Pāka'a, as a child, had raced against eight kānaka and beat them. But Pāka'a had a sail; Kūapāka'a didn't have one. Then he thought to himself, "If a big wave comes, I could ride it to shore."

He recalled his kupunawahine, La'amaomao. The famous wind gourd was his most trusty possession, but what he wanted right at the moment was a wave, so he chanted:

Ē La'amaomao,
Ē my kupunawahine,
Bring on, bring on a strong wind,
Raise the surf from Kahiki
To carry the canoe of your grandson to shore
The canoe of Kūapāka'a,
So we two will eat first our first mālolo.

When this chant ended, the wind blew, forming a swell, and in no time a big wave appeared. When Kūapāka'a saw the wave coming, he began to paddle with all his might. As his canoe caught the wave, the stern was lifted up high. He paddled strongly to catch the wave, then just steered with his paddle, letting the wave carry him. He wasn't worried about or afraid of damaging the canoe because it belonged to someone else, so even if it overturned or ran aground and cracked, it wasn't his loss. The most important thing to him was to land first and beat the other canoe.

When Kūapāka'a's canoe caught the big wave, the other canoe was near the entrance of the channel to shore, but when the men saw the huge wave rising up and feathering, they thought their canoe would be dashed against the reef, crushing them to death, so they stalled their canoe with their paddles to let the wave pass.

While they waited, they saw Kūapāka'a pass them and land. "The keiki has landed! The keiki has landed!" they shouted.

One of the keiki's companions said, "The keiki is really reckless.

He shouldn't have caught that huge, rough wave because he might have damaged the canoe, but he caught it anyway."

The other companion agreed: "Our dear canoe could have been smashed to bits, but he knew the canoe didn't belong to him and he wasn't responsible for it. All he cared about was winning our ka'au of fish."

After landing on the sandy beach, Kūapāka'a carried the canoe to the place where canoes were kept and then hid the fish inside the ali'i's canoe; then he waited calmly for the men to come ashore.

After the first big wave swept past, the other canoe wanted to enter the channel but another big wave followed, and then a third. When the sea was finally calm again, the men brought their canoe through the channel to shore.

While they were delayed by the waves, the keiki had taken and hidden all the fish.

When the other canoe landed, the kānaka asked the keiki, "Where's our fish?"

Kūapāka'a answered: "There's no fish left. I gave them all away to the kānaka. I knew I beat all of you, so all your ka'au of fish were mine— that's why I gave them away."

His answer was misleading since he hadn't given the fish away; he had hidden them.

The men were very angry because they had lost their fish. They had endured the chill of dawn, and fished until the sun had lost its red glow, but now they didn't have any fish to bring home and eat. They were so angry, they discussed having another race with the keiki to avenge their loss. Their bones would be the wager. After agreeing among themselves to this evil, perverse plan, they went and told Kūapāka'a, "Let's race again. You won because you rode a wave to shore. If you had to rely on paddling alone, you wouldn't have beaten us."

"That's perhaps just your opinion," said Kūapāka'a.

"'Ae, so let's race again," they said.

"'Ae, let's," said Kūapāka'a. "But there's one problem—we don't have anything of value to bet."

"Let's bet our bones. If we beat you, you'll be killed. If you beat us, we'll be killed."

"I don't want to wager our bones because if I beat you, you'll have to die, and your wives, children, and close friends will suffer. They'll weep and mourn over your deaths. I'm not afraid for myself. If you beat me, it would be all right for me to die because I'm just a keiki without any friends in this land. No one will mourn over me. But for you, it's different. So let's bet our goods instead of our bones. There's my bet—those double-hulled canoes resting there. If you beat me, those canoes are yours."

"Kā-hā-hā! Those aren't your canoes," said the kānaka. "Those canoes belong to the aliʻi; they belong to Keawenuiaʻumi."

"Those aren't his canoes," said Kūapākaʻa. "The people who ride on a canoe are merely passengers. The canoes belong to me because I watch over and care for them. I'm the guardian of these canoes. Where are the canoes of the people who live here? They only think these are their canoes."

"We don't want the canoes anyway," said the kānaka. "Let's wager our bodies."

"'Ae, why not?" said Kūapākaʻa. "But when I beat you and you must die, don't blame me—you're the ones who are insisting on betting our bones instead of our goods."

The kānaka said, "'Ae, since we've decided to race, let's race on the first day of Kau. The racing canoes must be six fathoms long and whoever loses will be baked in an imu."

"'Ae, we'll do whatever you want," said Kūapākaʻa.

The eight men racing against the keiki were the fishermen of the aliʻi Keawenuiaʻumi and close friends of Hoʻokele-i-Hilo and Hoʻokele-i-Puna. The two hoʻokele had appointed them as the fisherman of the aliʻi, replacing the previous fishermen, whom Pākaʻa had appointed. So Pākaʻa's appointees had lost their shares of the fishing to these new appointees.

After the rest of the fishing canoes landed, everyone returned home and praised the victory of the small keiki malihini over the fishermen of Keawenuiaʻumi. The news of the first race and the upcoming race between the fishermen and Kūapākaʻa circulated around the island of Hawaiʻi.

Although the news spread widely, Keawenuiaʻumi and the other kānaka who had gone in search of Pākaʻa still didn't remember the keiki who had brought them home. How incredible that this keiki malihini should have been so completely forgotten!

The upcoming race became publicized all over Hawaiʻi, and many people—men, women, and children—came to watch it. Not everyone thought the fishermen of Keawenuia'umi would win; some people backed Kūapāka'a.

Those on the keiki's side and those on the fishermen's side brought piles of goods to wager—what a huge collection of pua'a, 'īlio, hulu manu, kapa māmaki, kapa pa'ūpa'ū, and all kinds of other valuables!

Only a few people sided with the keiki; most of the people backed the fishermen of Keawenuia'umi; they felt the keiki couldn't win this race because he had to paddle a heavy canoe, six anana long, alone against eight men.

On the first day of the summer season of Kau, the fishermen of the ali'i carried the canoes down to the beach, then went to gather stones and firewood for an imu. The imu was dug and the wood was placed inside it, so it was ready to be lit.

Whoever lost the race would be thrown in; if the keiki won, the fishermen would be baked; if the fishermen won, the keiki would be baked.

As soon as the imu was ready, the men were eager to start the race, so they told the keiki, "Your imu is ready. Let's start."

"'A'ole," said Kūapāka'a. "First let's find two surfboards."

"What surfboards?" asked the kānaka. "We're having a canoe race."

"Here's my idea," said Kūapāka'a. "Before we go out and decide where to start the race, let's agree on how the race will end—let's say, whoever lands first must catch and ride four waves. If I get to shore first, I'll grab one of the surfboards and catch four waves, and if you haven't returned to shore yet, you clearly lose. If you reach shore first, one of you must grab one of the surfboards and ride four waves. If I haven't come to shore yet, then clearly, I've lost and must die. But of course, I'll lose since there are more of you."

"'Ae, let's go," they said.

The fishermen were in such a hurry to go, they didn't specify the kind of waves the first to shore had to catch—the shorebreak, or the waves that break farther out at sea and bring the rider to shore. Because the fishermen didn't specify which kind of waves, Kūapāka'a knew he would beat them one way or another.

The competitors boarded their canoes and paddled out to sea. After a while Kūapāka'a turned around and looked toward shore. The beach was hidden by the sea, so he called out to the other canoe, "Ē, how about here? Isn't this far enough out for you to outpaddle one person?"

"'A'ole, let's paddle farther out—until the hale are hidden by the sea. Then we'll start," said the kānaka.

"It's pointless to go farther out," said Kūapāka'a. "There are eight of you—why are you afraid of just one little keiki? If we had started the race just outside the breaking waves, you would have easily beaten me. But no, you want to go farther out, so now I'm telling you I'll beat you. I pity your wives, children, and parents."

They paddled farther out; after a short while, the kānaka turned around and looked toward shore. The hale were almost hidden by the sea, so they called to Kūapāka'a, "Here—this is a good starting point."

"'Ae, it'll do," said Kūapāka'a.

They stopped the canoes and lined them up, and when the canoes were even, the kānaka called out, "We're even. Start paddling!"

The fishermen began paddling with all their might, each trying to outpaddle the others thinking he would be the one to win the race. Thus, their paddling wasn't in unison. At the start of the race, the fishermen's canoe surged ahead, but Kūapāka'a noticed their paddling wasn't efficient like the paddling of canoe-racers: when the fishermen drew their paddles out of the water, the sea was churned up with froth.

Kūapāka'a also noticed the rushing wake behind the other canoe, so he paddled strongly to catch the wave it created; once he caught the wave, all he had to do was steer his canoe with his paddle.

While the kānaka in the other canoe wasted their strength paddling hard, Kūapāka'a enjoyed riding their wake without paddling and without falling behind.

One of them glanced back and saw the bow of the keiki's canoe just behind the stern of their canoe, so they continued to paddle with all their might. When Kūapāka'a saw them looking at him, he called out, "Ē, paddle harder or you'll lose. Here I am—right behind you."

The men didn't bother to answer as they concentrated on paddling. As the two canoes got closer to shore, the crowd saw the canoe with the eight kānaka in front and began shouting, "Here comes the canoe of the ali'i's fishermen! Here comes the canoe of the ali'i's fishermen!!"

The people on shore who had bet on the fishermen began boasting about the fishermen's victory over the keiki and the goods they would win.

Since the keiki's canoe was right behind the fishermen's canoe, the people on shore couldn't see it and didn't realize the keiki's canoe was so close behind.

The canoes had started racing from a long way out, so after a while the eight men were very exhausted: they perspired profusely, their arms began to stiffen, their breathing became labored, and their bodies ached. One of them had to lie down in the canoe, unable to paddle any more. Another put his paddle down and bowed his head forward. When the others saw the distress of these two, they began to feel their own paddling was a waste of effort.

Kūapākaʻa saw the men giving up, so he paddled hard to leave the wake of the other canoe and draw his canoe even with theirs.

When the men saw the keiki's canoe had caught up to theirs, they tried to paddle with renewed vigor, but in vain because they were so exhausted.

Kūapākaʻa paddled strongly and moved ahead of the other canoe.

When those who backed the keiki saw his canoe emerge from behind the other canoe, they cried out, "The keiki's pulling ahead! The keiki's pulling ahead!!"

There was a great commotion among the people on shore as the keiki's canoe emerged from behind the other canoe. Those who bet on him cheered, while the others were sullen and silent, regretting the anticipated loss of their goods to those who bet on the keiki.

Kūapākaʻa's canoe kept moving farther ahead, while the other canoe fell farther behind. Thus the keiki reached shore first. He quickly jumped off his canoe, grabbed one of the surfboards, ran back to the sea, and caught four waves breaking on the sandy beach. He had defeated the fishermen of Keawenuiaʻumi.

When the keiki was back on shore, a din arose among the crowd. Those who had backed the keiki leaped for joy, shouting, "The keiki's won! The keiki's won!!"

The fishermen were very surprised when they saw Kūapākaʻa quickly catch four waves near shore. They thought they still had time to beat the keiki because they assumed they had agreed to catch four waves at sea, not four waves near shore.

They realized their mistake—they hadn't made clear what kind of waves had to be caught when the keiki spoke to them about adding surfing to the contest. They had agreed to the vague terms, so they couldn't argue now. When they came ashore, they sat quietly, regretting that they had insisted on wagering their bones. The imu for baking them had been lit; fear of dying gripped their chests, and they felt sorrow for their wives, children, parents, and close friends.

They watched the keiki's backers gather up the winnings.

The news of fishermen's defeat reached the aloali'i of Keawenuia'umi; a kahu who heard the news went to tell the ali'i.

"What brings you here?" the ali'i asked the kahu.

"I came to tell you the results of a canoe race."

"Who raced?" the ali'i asked.

"Some of your kānaka raced against a keiki malihini.

"What was the wager?"

"Their bones—if the keiki won, your kānaka would be baked in an imu; if your kānaka won, the keiki would be baked."

"Who won?"

"The keiki."

"Where is the keiki?"

"At the beach."

"Where are my kānaka?"

"At the beach, hunkered down. Their wives, children, and close friends are lamenting their fate."

The ali'i began recalling earlier events and asked, "Is the keiki small?"

"'Ae, he's a small keiki."

"Kā! If it's the same keiki who sailed with us from Moloka'i, he couldn't have been beaten."

For the first time since returning to Hawai'i, Keawenui-a'umi remembered the keiki; then he ordered his kahu, "Go and look for the keiki, and when you find him, tell him, 'Keawenuia'umi orders you to appear before him.' I want to see if he's perhaps the same keiki who sailed with us."

The ali'i's kahu found Kūapāka'a at the beach and told him, "Keawenuia'umi orders you to appear before him."

"'Ae, let's go." Kūapāka'a went with the kahu and appeared before Keawenuia'umi. The ali'i saw he was indeed the very same keiki who accompanied him on his search for Pāka'a, the one who had saved him from death at sea and guided his canoe back to Hawai'i.

The ali'i said, "Come, come here."

"I'm not worthy to enter your kapu area, my ali'i," said Kūapāka'a.

"The kapu is lifted for you," said Keawenuia'umi.

The keiki crawled forward on his hands and knees, and when he reached Keawenuia'umi, the ali'i embraced the keiki around the neck, kissed him, and cried out lovingly for him. His love for the keiki welled up in him, and his tears fell. He remembered all the excellent work the keiki had done for him, and he felt remorse over having forgotten the keiki who had saved him twice from danger and death.

After the ali'i's tears of joy and regret stopped flowing, he ordered his 'āipu'upu'u to bring quickly 'ai and i'a for the keiki. A fine feast was prepared, and savory dishes, fine foods, and rich, fatty delicacies usually reserved for the ali'i were served to the keiki.

As the keiki ate, Keawenuia'umi asked, "Where have you been living?"

"Our canoe has been my hale, and the leftovers from our voyage have been my food."

"Auwē! I urged you to sail with me, but back here, you've been sadly neglected. I assumed some of our people would take care of you, but I was wrong."

The ali'i again lamented his neglect of the keiki: "Auwē, I've been neglectful. Our reward to you after you brought us back home safely was to abandon you as a malihini at the beach. Yet if it weren't for you, the bones of the main branch of the royal family would be at the bottom of the ocean."

While recounting the keiki's past deeds, the ali'i expressed his deep gratitude. Then he told the keiki, "When you predicted you were going to be neglected once the canoe was carried ashore, you were right. No one, not even I, took you in."

After his burdensome concern for the keiki was lightened, Keawenuia'umi remembered that his fishermen would soon be put to death. The ali'i asked the keiki, "Aren't you the one who raced against my kānaka in Kohala?"

"'Ae, I'm he."

"What was the wager?"

"In our first race, the wager was fish, and I won; in the second race, the wager was our bones, and I won again. When I left the beach, the imu fire was being lit. The wives, children, and close friends of the losers were weeping. When the imu is hot enough, I plan to return there and have the fishermen thrown in."

Once again Keawenuia'umi shed tears, bowing his head while weeping.

Kūapāka'a asked him, "Why does the ali'i weep?"

"I weep for my kānaka."

"Kā, it's not my fault. I urged them to bet our belongings. They asked what I had to wager, and I pointed to our canoes, but they refused to take the bet. They stubbornly insisted on wagering our bones in this race. They were angry at me, so they wanted to defeat me and have me killed."

"Listen, ē ke keiki, you've shown great love for me and helped me evade death twice. So how do you feel toward me now? If your love for me is still strong, I'm asking you to spare my kānaka because I would prefer that they live. I would be at a loss without them—they know where the fish are in the ocean and how to catch them. Without these kānaka, I wouldn't have any fish. If what I've said makes you feel any pity for me, then allow them to live; if not, it's better that you kill me."

"I feel love for you, my ali'i, but I regret I have to refuse your request. I can't give in to your appeal; I have a good reason to see these fishermen killed. But to make things right, how about if I leave the life or death of your kānaka up to you?"

Kūapāka'a continued, "Ē ke ali'i, forgive this kanaka for asking rudely, but do you regret the loss of these kānaka more than the loss of any other kanaka?"

"'Ae, I regret having to ask you to spare them, but if they're killed, I'm afraid the fishing would go badly. I wouldn't regret their loss so much if I had found my kauwā—if I had found Pāka'a and brought him home with me. But we never found Pāka'a, so I'd be deprived of my supply of fish if these kānaka were killed."

Kūapāka'a answered, "If you value the lives of these kānaka so highly, Pāka'a will never return here, even if we went to get him on Ka'ula. But if you allow me to kill these kānaka, you'll see your former kauwā again. It was because you had so many new favorites that you neglected Pāka'a and treated him with contempt. That's how you hurt your kauwā, so he left you. Now you be the one to choose whether Pāka'a returns or not."

"If what you say is true, go and get Pāka'a and when I see him, I'll let you put these men to death," said the ali'i.

When the ali'i made this promise, Kūapāka'a knew his father's last enemies would die, so he thought the time was right to reveal Pāka'a's whereabouts. He told the ali'i, "Do you remember when we first met, and I told you a storm was coming and you would die at sea if you didn't follow my advice?"

"'Ae, I remember."

"Pāka'a was in the small shelter at the bow of my canoe."

"Auwē, so that was he!"

"'Ae, he kept his head down because he knew if you saw him, you would urge him to return to Hawai'i with you, but he would still be at the mercy of his enemies, your new favorites. I'm his keiki, Kūapāka'a. He named me for you, for your scaly, 'awa-dried skin. He taught me all the things he once did for you, so I was able to perform his duties when we were at sea."

Keawenuia'umi wondered, "Are you telling the truth, ē ke keiki?"

"'Ae, it's true," said Kūapāka'a. "I was allowed to sail with you to kill my father's enemies and avenge his betrayal."

Keawenuia'umi felt excitment and happiness about the possibility of finding Pāka'a again, but he still harbored a small doubt, so he didn't respond right away. Because the ali'i paused a long while before answering, Kūapāka'a said, "Ē ke ali'i, I know I can't prove beyond any doubt my words are true. All I can say is: believe me. If not, then so be it. Here's the truth: the malo I gave you on Moloka'i, which surprised you, was indeed your malo, and so was the kapa I gave you. But Pāka'a told me to tell you they were mine."

After hearing this, the ali'i was certain the keiki was telling the truth. Then he wept aloud for the keiki and Pāka'a. When his lamentation ended, he decided the fate of the fishermen: they had to be killed.

The ali'i sent for his ilāmuku and gave an order to have the fishermen killed, as had been specified in the wager with the keiki—the kānaka were to be thrown into the fiery imu and burned to death.

They had tried to kill the keiki, but they would be put to death instead.

As soon as the ilāmuku left, the ali'i told Kūapāka'a, "Ē ke keiki, go now to Moloka'i and tell Pāka'a all his enemies are dead, so he should return immediately to look after me. I have no kānaka left—no ho'okele, no lawai'a."

"'Ae, I'll go and get him," said Kūapāka'a.

The ali'i commanded his kānaka to prepare one of the canoes for the keiki and when it was ready, he ordered some of his hoewa'a, "Go with the boy to find my kauwā and bring him back."

Kūapāka'a responded, "'A'ole, I'll go alone to bring Pāka'a back."

At dawn the next day, Kūapāka'a sailed for Moloka'i. When the sun was overhead, he arrived at Ho'olehua, Moloka'i, the land of his birth.

When Keawenuia'umi's canoe had left Moloka'i with Kūapāka'a on board, Pāka'a and Hikauhi remained behind with just the memory of their keiki. While they waited, longing for her keiki welled up in Hikauhi because from infancy, he had never been apart from them. She tried to suppress her longing for him, but couldn't, so she got angry at Pāka'a and began scolding him for letting their keiki leave: "You know I love my keiki, yet you sent him away with your haku. Perhaps my keiki has drowned at sea and won't return. What was the purpose of hiding yourself from your haku if my keiki isn't going to return? If my keiki hadn't been taken to Ka'ula because you misled your ali'i to go and find you there, perhaps my keiki wouldn't have been lost at sea."

"The keiki isn't dead," said Pāka'a. "He'll come back soon. Let's look forward to that day. Soon we'll see a single canoe coming from the east, from the direction of Maui, and it'll be our keiki. I let him sail with Keawenuia'umi so he could avenge me during the voyage; it would make me very happy to know that the two ho'okele are dead and that my keiki has returned to Hawai'i and killed their fishermen to redeem my honor. Then all of the ali'i's new favorites will have been destroyed, and once all my enemies are gone, I'll be able to return home and live a good life again with my haku."

In spite of Pāka'a's words, Hikauhi was still angry and she kept on badgering Pāka'a every day. However, she spent most of her time watching the swells of the sea of Pailolo, yearning to see her keiki again.

One day as Pāka'a and Hikauhi watched together, he saw a small canoe sailing on the ocean; he turned to his wife and said, "Here's your keiki, returning home."

"Where?" asked Hikauhi.

"There, see that small white speck on the ocean?"

"'Ae, there."

"'Ae, that's he—let's not lose sight of the sail of his canoe. He's killed the two ho'okele, then returned to Hawai'i with my haku. He remained there for a while, but now he's returning to us."

When Kūapāka'a's canoe came closer, Hikauhi went down to the canoe landing to wait for the keiki. As soon as the canoe touched the sand, Kūapāka'a stood up, went to the bow of the canoe, and leaped onto the beach. Hikauhi rushed to her keiki, and began hugging and kissing him; her mind was finally at rest because she could look into his eyes again.

Kūapāka'a carried his canoe onto land, and when it was properly placed and cared for, he returned to the kauhale.

When he arrived at the kauhale, Pāka'a quickly asked, "How was your trip? Did it go well?"

"'Ae, it went well. The two ho'okele and your haku's favorite fishermen are dead." Kūapāka'a recounted the events from the time he left Moloka'i until his return.

Then he said to his father, "I told your haku about you and me, and he sent me to bring you back with this command: 'Tell Pāka'a all his enemies are dead, so he should return immediately to look after me since now I don't have any kānaka left—no ho'okele-wa'a, no lawai'a.' So now let's board the canoe and sail back to Hawai'i."

Pāka'a asked the keiki, "Have the rights to any of your haku's lands been granted to you?

"No properties have been granted to me; all he said was that I should come to get you."

Pāka'a told the keiki, "You're ignorant about how such things are done. Would that you had obtained some of my moku, ahupua'a, and kalana perhaps—here he's been most neglectful."

"I know if I made a request, some rights could be obtained," said the keiki. "I'm assuming the ali'i knows what's fair for the kanaka, and he'll grant rights to the kanaka."

"That's not so, ē ke keiki; when the ali'i urged you to come for me, that's when I would have asked for rights on behalf of the kanaka and, my rights recognized, I would return to the aloali'i wealthy and prosperous. If things remain for us as they are, what we have here on Moloka'i is good enough, with the sky above and the earth below. We're well off and live like ali'i on this island."

"Then perhaps it was wrong to have killed off the lawai'a and ho'okele-wa'a of the ali'i; his life is truly destitute."

Pāka'a replied, "If that's so, go back to Hawai'i and tell your ali'i, 'Pāka'a said when you return the lands which were taken from him earlier, and when you restore all the rights that were previously his, he'll return. If not, he won't come back.'"

"'Ae, after I've rested, I'll go back to Hawai'i to do what's right for us." The keiki ate until he was full, then fell asleep.

The keiki rested for two days; on the third day, he prepared to sail back to Hawai'i to seek rights on behalf of his father and himself.

Meanwhile, Keawenuia'umi had waited until the evening of the second day for Pāka'a to return to Hawai'i, and when he didn't, the ali'i sent an 'elele for Kahikuokamoku, the Kuhina Nui.

The 'elele found Kahikuokamoku and told him, "The ali'i has sent me to summon you right away."

"Is that so? What is his command?"

"He didn't say."

They went together to the ali'i, and the ali'i told Kahikuokamoku, "Prepare a canoe quickly and go to Moloka'i to ask about Pāka'a. The keiki told me Pāka'a is indeed there. I sent the keiki to get him, but the keiki still hasn't returned."

"'Ae, your orders will be obeyed," said Kahikuokamoku; he commanded some kānaka to secure the lashings of a canoe and prepare for the trip.

At dawn on the third day after Kūapāka'a had left, Kahikuokamoku and the hoewa'a boarded the canoe and set off for Moloka'i. Before the sun was directly overhead, they reached Ho'olehua. Kūapāka'a had just finished preparing his canoe to return to Hawai'i and was back at the kauhale when some kānaka shouted, "A canoe is coming! A canoe is coming!!"

Pāka'a saw the canoe enter the harbor and said to his keiki, "They're looking for you. The ali'i waited for us, and when we didn't come right away, he sent out a canoe to find us. You stay here while I go to your kūpuna's place; I'll return with the kūpuna this evening."

Kūapāka'a waited calmly while the canoe landed and was carried up and placed on the beach. Then Kahikuokamoku and the hoewa'a went inland and reached the kauhale. Kūapāka'a welcomed them and they greeted him; then they all ate until they were full and sat around enjoying themselves.

While they were relaxing, Kūapāka'a asked Kahikuokamoku, "What is your destination?"

"Here."

"What's the reason for your visit?"

"To find Pāka'a," said Kahikuokamoku. "The ali'i waited for two days and when you didn't return with Pāka'a, he sent me to bring the two of you back. Where is Pāka'a?"

"I haven't found him yet because I'm expecting a malihini to arrive here this evening and I have to wait for him."

"How soon will this malihini get here?"

"At any time—he may be on his way now."

Before the evening meal, Kūapāka‘a had sent an ‘elele to tell Pāka‘a and Hikauhi and all the others to come and present gifts to Kahikuokamoku, the Kuhina Nui of Keawenuia‘umi, so the people of Hawai‘i would know that Kūapāka‘a was a native child of this land.

While the people of Hawai‘i waited with the keiki for the malihini, the people of Moloka‘i began arriving and giving gifts. They brought with them things of value such as kapa, ‘ai and i‘a, pua‘a, ‘īlio, and other forms of wealth acquired by those of ancient times. The first to give gifts were the many who lived in Pāka‘a’s household; their ‘ōhua preceded them; behind the crowd were Pāka‘a and Hikauhi.

After the gift-giving was over, Pāka‘a and Hikauhi arrived with Ho‘olehua and ‘Īloli, Hikauhi’s parents, and her brother, Kaumanamana.

Pāka‘a stood for a while outside the doorway until Lapakahoe turned toward the doorway and saw him; he stood up quickly, shouting, "It’s Pāka‘a! It’s Pāka‘a!!" He ran outside and met Pāka‘a, and they embraced each other, weeping for love and joy.

When the people of Hawai‘i heard Lapakahoe’s shouts, they all scrambled to their feet and rushed outside. Kahikuokamoku was first, followed by the hoewa‘a; and all of them also wept with joy.

After the tears had dried, everyone relaxed and enjoyed the rest of the evening. The people of Hawai‘i told Pāka‘a about the deeds of his keiki from the time they had left Moloka‘i until the time they landed on Hawai‘i.

While they were relaxing, Kahikuokamoku said, "So you were here all the time. Why did you conceal yourself from your haku? We exhausted ourselves looking for you, and we almost drowned at sea; some actually did drown. I pitied the ali‘i because he had to endure the cold and other hardships at sea. The bones of your haku were almost lost while looking for you in vain."

"‘Ae, my haku almost died at sea, but he didn’t. The ali‘i gave the stern of his canoe to Ho‘okele-i-Hilo and Ho‘okele-i-Puna because of their supposed expertise in navigation; and because of my supposed incompetence, I was just pushed aside, my position at the stern of the canoe unjustly usurped. But you know the truth—we’ve sailed together with the ali‘i many times and went together everywhere with Keawenuia‘umi, my haku, my ali‘i. You’ve never known him to be in danger at sea; only when you and he sailed without me did you face such danger."

"'Ae, you're right. After almost drowning at sea, the ali'i praised your skill in navigation and sailing, and told us 'My buttocks wouldn't be wet if Pāka'a were with me—because you are all incompetent, my buttocks are wet.'"

Some time later Kahikuokamoku added, "So this one who came sailing with us is your keiki?"

"'Ae, he's my keiki, I won't deny him because he carried out my revenge exactly as I told him to."

Then Pāka'a pointed to Hikauhi and said, "This is the keiki's mother, the woman I married while I lived as a malihini here on Moloka'i." Hikauhi and Kahikuokamoku greeted each other.

After the two conversed, Kahikuokamoku turned to Pāka'a to urge him to return: "Ē Pāka'a, it's good that I've found you here, so now let's return to Hawai'i, as your hānai has commanded."

"If the position at the stern of the canoe is restored to me, along with all the lands and rights taken from me, I'll return," said Pāka'a.

"All these things will be given back to you if you return." said Kahikuokamoku.

"'Ae, then I'll return, but not right away," said Pāka'a. "You go back first to our ali'i and tell him what I've said. After he recognizes my rights, then I'll return; after he grants me all that belongs to me, then he should send for me and my household again. Only the keiki will go with you at this time."

"'Ae, you're right," Kahikuokamoku said. Then he ordered the hoewa'a to secure the lashings of the canoe and prepare it quickly for sea. When all was ready, Pāka'a loaded on board some gifts and some of the ali'i's personal things which he had kept in his care. Then Kahikuokamoku returned to Hawai'i with Kūapāka'a.

They left at dawn and when the sun was descending, they landed on Hawai'i. Kahikuokamoku and Kūapāka'a went before Keawenuia'umi. When the ali'i saw Kūapāka'a, he greeted the keiki cheerfully because he thought Pāka'a had also returned; but when he didn't see Pāka'a, he asked: "Did you find Pāka'a?"

"'Ae, we found him," said Kahikuokamoku. "He sent these gifts to you and returned some of the personal things he's kept for you all this time; these are proof he was really found."

"Where is he?"

"Living on Moloka'i," said Kahikuokamoku.

"Why hasn't he returned?"

"He sent me to request that you return to him all that is rightfully his," answered Kahikuokamoku. "His words were 'If the position of navigator is restored to me along with all the lands and rights taken from me, I'll return.' If you refuse, he won't return; if you agree, send for him and he'll return."

"I didn't even think about what was right for my kahu. Return quickly to Moloka'i, and tell him I agree to restore to him the lands once granted to him, as well as all the rights that were once his."

A few days later the ali'i said to Kahikuokamoku, "Order the people to provide two hundred canoes to bring Pāka'a and all his 'ōhua back here to Hawai'i. Meanwhile, the keiki will stay with me."

"'Ae," said Kahikuokamoku. The people were told to provide the canoes, and in no time, there were enough canoes. After the canoes were made ready, Kahikuokamoku once again left for Moloka'i to bring Pāka'a back.

One day while Pāka'a was watching the sea, he saw the canoe fleet coming over the sea of Pailolo, like a school of mālolo churning the ocean into foam.

He called Hikauhi over and pointed out the canoe fleet: "Here they come to take us back to Hawai'i."

"Indeed, we'll return to Hawai'i and live in your glory," said Hikauhi.

Soon the canoes came through the channel and were carried up on land. Kahikuokamoku went ashore quickly and found Pāka'a, and after they greeted one another, Kahikuokamoku spoke: "The ali'i has agreed to restore to you the position at the stern of the canoe, along with your former lands and rights. So let's return."

"'Ae, let's return." Pāka'a then told all the members of his 'ohana to prepare to go to Hawai'i. His 'ōhua and the many who wanted to go and live with him on Hawai'i as well as those who just wanted to go sightseeing got ready and boarded the canoes. They all went to Hawai'i. On this voyage, Pāka'a travelled like an ali'i, taking with him all his 'ōhua and the many others who lived with him during his stay on Moloka'i.

When Pāka'a's company arrived on Hawai'i, Pāka'a appeared before Keawenuia'umi, and the ali'i rushed to embrace him while lamenting his mistreatment of his excellent kauwā.

After they expressed their deep love for one another, and the lamentations subsided, they told one another what each had done and asked each other about things that had happened during their separation; and all was well.

The days of Pākaʻa's separation from his hānai were over. Keawenuiaʻumi told Pākaʻa, "It's good that you're back; I reappoint you to your former position, grant you all of your former lands and rights, and give you the care and supervision of the island of Hawaiʻi."

Thus, Pākaʻa was victorious over his enemies who had come between him and his hānai. With the help of Kūapākaʻa, his keiki, Pākaʻa returned to enjoy the comforts and honors and carry out the responsibilities of an aliʻi of Hawaiʻi.

KA HOPENA

NOTES

1. Keawenuia'umi ruled the island of Hawai'i during the 16th century. His father, 'Umi, was famous for uniting all the districts of Hawai'i under one rule after his men killed his brother Hakau, who had a purer chiefly bloodline and a higher right to rule the kingdom. ('Umi's mother, Akahi-a-Kuleana, was of low chiefly birth.)

Keawenuia'umi's mother, Kapukini, was 'Umi's half sister, whom 'Umi married to keep as much chiefly mana (power) in his offspring as possible. After 'Umi died, the island of Hawai'i was divided between two of his sons: Keawenuia'umi was given the lands Hilo, and his older brother, Keli'iokaloa, was given the lands of Kona. Keli'iokaloa's subjects were unhappy with their ali'i's oppressive, impious rule and some of them went to Hilo to offer Kona to Keawenuia'umi. After Keawenuia'umi's forces defeated Keli'iokaloa's forces in battle and killed Keli'iokaloa, Keawenuia'umi established his rule over the whole island. (See Kamakau's *Ruling Chiefs* for the stories of 'Umi and Keawenuia'umi.)

The Wind Gourd of La'amaomao portrays Keawenuia'umi as a good-hearted, but weak and gullible leader. The heroes of the legend are three generations of kahu iwikuamo'o, or "backbone attendants," who served Keawenuia'umi. The kahu iwikuamo'o was a close relative of an ali'i who handled the personal effects, needs, and affairs of the ruling chief. (Only a close relative with chiefly blood could handle such things because everything about the ali'i, including his body, food, and clothing, were taboo.) The story is told from the point of view of the kahu and emphasizes the importance of good servants in running a government efficiently and taking care of a weak ali'i.

2. Favorite children were often carried so they wouldn't have to walk and were not allowed to do work that soiled their hands or to carry anything heavy in their hands or on their shoulders (Kamakau, *The People* 26-7).

3. Saying 1677 in Mary Kawena Pukui's *'Ōlelo No'eau* reads: *"Ke ali'i nana e kālua i ke po'o i ka imu a po'alo a'e i na maka.* The chief who can roast the head in the imu and scoop out the eyes. Said of a chief who had the power and authority to have the head of one who offended him cut off and roasted in an imu or to order his eyes dug out. The heads were roasted and then discarded as a warning to lesser chiefs and commoners to respect their superiors."

4. Giving this rather strange name to his offspring is apparently an act of humility and self-abasement on the part of the kahu. The kahu often refers to

himself as his aliʻiʻs kauwā, or slave. Panaʻewa is an upland area of the Hilo district on the Big Island; ʻawa is a plant from whose roots a mild narcotic drink was made.

5. It was customary in Hawaiʻi for the first-born child to be reared by the grandparents or some other relative: "The parents did not rear their own child; its rearing was in the hands of the grandparents or their younger or older brothers and sisters, or other lateral relatives (hoahanau), or in the hands of the lateral relatives of the parents." Male children usually went to the father's side of the family; female children to the mother's side (Kamakau, The People 26).

6. "It was well known that the chiefs, as a class, were physically larger than the masses, so much so that they claimed ... a descent distinct from that of the common people" (Kalākaua 106).

7. Kaʻelo (May-June) was when the first mālolo was eaten and "mālolo was so plentiful that fishermen's containers were full to the brim" (Kamakau, The Works 15). Titcomb says March–June is the best season for mālolo fishing.

8. The kai mālolo ("sea where mālolo is caught") is located between the kai lu heʻe, ("sea where octopi were caught," "just before the sea becomes very dark") and the koʻa hi kāhala and koʻa hi ʻahi, the deep sea fishing ground for kāhala (amberjack) and ʻahi (yellow-fin tuna) (Kamakau, The Works 11).

9. "For mālolo fishing, a double canoe or a large single one carrying the hano [a large bag net of a very fine mesh, with a flaring mouth] and an attending fleet from 20 to 40 canoes make an early morning start. Women very often go in this kind of fishing to help paddle the canoes as no particular skill is called for on the part of the general hands, the success of the fishing depending altogether on the good judgment and sight of the kilo (lookout). This person generally rides on a light canoe manned by only two or three paddlers, and he is always standing up on the cross ties of the canoe looking for the mālolo; whenever he discerns a strong ripple, he points it out to the rest of the canoes, which then surround the spot indicated while the kilo confers with the head fishermen about the best place to drop the hano, depending on the direction of the current; when the net is ready, the canoes paddle very quickly in toward it, splashing the water and driving the fish before them into the open net. It seems these fish will not dive to any depth and are always found swimming very near the surface, so, when completely surrounded by canoes, they can be driven wherever wanted. The fleet very often goes several miles out to sea after mālolo, and this fishing is called one of the lawaia-o-kaiuli, or blue-sea fishing" (Beckley 17-18).

108

10. 'Uko'a is a fishpond in Waialua, O'ahu. According to the Pukui-Elbert *Hawaiian Dictionary*, "The fish of 'Uko'a have vanished" (Pupuhi ka i'a o 'Uko'a) refers to "one who flees." According to Henry P. Judd's *Hawaiian Proverbs and Riddles* (1930), the fish of 'Uko'a are hard to get and the phrase is said of something difficult to catch. Pāka'a is alluding to both himself and the catch of fish, which are now out of reach of the fishermen.

11. In describing the traditional Hawaiian house, or hale, Malo writes, "Some people...sponged [ka ho'opili wale] on those who had houses [ka po'e mea hale]. Such [sponges] were called o-kea-pili-mai ["drift gravel"] or unu-pehi-'iole ["rat-pelting pebbles"]. These were names of reproach [lapuwale, or "worthless"]. But that was not the way people of respectability [lapuwale 'ole] lived. They put up houses of their own" (118).

12. A similar father-son recognition scene occurs in the story of 'Umi-a-Liloa, Keawenuia'umi's father. Like Pāka'a, 'Umi-a-Liloa seeks out his father at the royal court in Waipi'o Valley. Like Pāka'a, 'Umi enters the royal compound and sits on his father's lap: "The boy had broken another tabu. The chief looked at the boy sitting on his lap and asked, 'Whose child are you?' The boy answered, 'Yours! I am 'Umi-a-Liloa.' Liloa noticed the tokens he had left for his son and kissed and wept over him" (Kamakau, *Ruling Chiefs* 7). The Pāka'a story presents the parallel between Pāka'a and 'Umi in order to help establish Pāka'a's right to the position of kahu iwikuamo'o held by his father Kūanu'uanu: even though Pāka'a, like 'Umi, has been born to a country woman of lower status than his father, he is able to obtain his father's position through his superior ability.

13. Cf. the advice given to John Papa Ii by his mother: "' ... you must think of that man and this man, that boy and this boy, that chief and this chief, that you may act rightly. Thus does the uncle for whom you are named. He serves all the chiefs in the court, where you are going to live'" (Ii 27). Ii's uncle was a kahu to Kamehameha I, and Ii was trained from youth to serve in the court of the Kamehamehas. Ii's mother is telling her son not to seek revenge against a boy who has injured one of Ii's friends: "'To be tolerant is best.'" However, as the story of Pāka'a makes clear, revenge was considered just in pre-Christian Hawai'i.

14. These two names mean "Navigator-to-Hilo" and "Navigator-to-Puna"; the names suggest the limited ability of these two ho'okele; each knows the route to only one place, so they must share the position of navigator; Pāka'a knows the winds of all the islands and can navigate the ali'i's canoe anywhere among them.

15. The names of these Moloka'i people are place names of south-central

Moloka'i. Pāka'a's house site is located west of Kaumanamana in the district of Kaluako'i. See the map of Moloka'i at the end of the text.

16. "E momole aku ana Keka'a ka ua nahua"—"The pelting rains wears down ["wears smooth"] the rock of Keka'a." This saying is not found in Pukui's *'Ōlelo No'eau*. It seems to mean, "Continual efforts result in achieving one's goal". According to *Place Names of Hawaii* (Pukui, Elbert, and Mookini), Keka'a is a rock and an area near Kā'anapali, Maui, and literally means "the rumble," as in a thunderstorm. Nahua is a wind associated with Kā'anapali.

17. Canoe-carvers often watched the behavior of birds around a tree to determine if the tree was solid or rotten inside. According to the Pukui-Elbert *Hawaiian Dictionary*, "an elepaio pecking slowly on a tree trunk for insects signified that the trunk was insect-ridden and not suitable for a canoe." The elepaio is actually a flycatcher rather than a woodpecker, capable of catching insects in the air beneath the forest canopy, though it also feeds on insects in the foliage and bark of tree. In the story of Pāka'a, the chirping of the two supernatural birds causes the trees to be rotten.

18. The legend of Pikoiaka'alalā and his famous feats of archery is told in Fornander's *Hawaiian Antiquities and Folk-lore*, Vol. 4, and in William D. Westervelt's *Hawaiian Legends of Old Honolulu*.

19. Ka'ula is a rocky islet 22 miles southwest of Kaua'i. It was thought of as the westernmost land of ancient Hawai'i; uninhabited today except by birds, it is said to have a heiau on its western side and was believed to have been the home of a shark god.

20. Pāka'a's sweet potato patches and sugar cane fields were located "in a straight line from the upland of Punahou [*sic*] to the summit on the west side of the disk-(*maika*) playing site of Maunaloa. The sweet-potato and sugar cane patches were about a mile long and about half a mile wide. Pāka'a did his farming in the winter months when there was an abundance of rain. The plains were made fertile when the rain fell. The soil at the top of Maunaloa was composed of light gravel and ash, and sweet potatoes and sugar cane flourished. His production was great" (Kamakau, *Ruling Chiefs* 42). Handy and Handy note "Southwest of Mauna Loa in Punakou District is the site of Pāka'a's house and his potato plantations famous in legend. Phelps, in his field notes, refers to Kaluakoi, 'just south of Amikopala,' as the traditional site of Pāka'a's sweet-potato patch" (517).

21. The days of Kū were the first three days of the 29.5 lunar month (Hilo, Hoaka, and Kū-kahi), so called because these days were kapu for the god Kū. It was the duty of the priests, the astrologers, the soothsayers, and the

navigators to predict the days of good weather for sailing by interpreting natural signs and dreams.

22. To catch uhu, or parrot fish, the fisherman used a live decoy tied to a string to lure other fish into a hand-held net. Kamakau describes this expert method of fishing: "The fisherman was most likely a mature man, with bleached eyebrows, and eyes obscured by deposits of salt. His head was underwater as he watched closely for fish; his ears were 'racks' (*haka*) for *kukui* nut meat and his mouth would spew forth chewed *kukui* meat which becalmed the sea so that he could see the bottom. One hand of the fisherman directed the movements of the decoy *uhu*, and his left hand sculled (*koali*) the paddle inside the *ama* to keep the nose of the canoe headed into the wind" (*The Works* 65). According to Kamakau, the uhu fishing ground of Pāka'a was off Kala'au Point, at the southwestern tip of Moloka'i (*Ruling Chiefs* 38).

23. The appearance of royalty was often associated with a blaze of fire; or these fires could be cooking fires on board the canoes.

24. Kaukauali'i: a class of chiefs of lesser rank than the ruling chief; a chief whose father was a high chief and whose mother was of lower rank but not a commoner. The ali'i of old Hawai'i enjoyed belittling the ancestry of rival ali'i who were competing for power, privileges, or favors at court. The insults might include, as they do here, defaming the land which a rival ali'i ruled. By calling the district ali'i "kaukauali'i," Pāka'a seems to be alluding to the fact that after Keawenuia'umi defeated and killed his brother in battle and established his rule over the whole island, he redistributed the lands to his most loyal relatives, who did not necessarily have the highest chiefly rights to rule (as determined by blood lines); hence, the belittling of the social status of the district ali'i in these chants. Handy and Handy note, "The custom of redistributing land rights among *ali'i* upon the accession of the new *mo'i* [king] dates traditionally from the time of Keawenuia'umi of Waipi'o, Hawai'i, reckoned as eleven generations preceding Kamehameha the Great" (45).

25. Kohala was famous of its sugar cane, and its warriors were compared to the "resistant white sugar cane." See Pukui's *'Ōlelo No'eau*, Sayings No. 875 and 1171. 'Uhini, or grasshoppers, were strung on stems and broiled as food (Handy and Handy 259).

26. Eel-catching by hand in shallow water and on reefs was not considered an expert way of fishing; it was "just for the taking of fish to make living more pleasurable—to have something for the family and guests to eat with their poi. Superior to these ways were fishing with long lines and by diving" (Kamakau, *The Works* 59-60). Thus, Kuapāka'a insults Wanu'a here by

calling him a mere eel-catcher. See Kamakau for a description of eel-catching with the hand (*The Works* 86-7).

27. The insult used by Kuapāka'a here is proverbial: "Waiakea pepeiao pulu 'aha," translated "Waiakea of the ears that hold coconut-fiber snares." Pukui explains in *'Ōlelo No 'eau*: "Snares for small fish, shrimp, or crabs were made of a coconut midrib and the fiber from the husk of the nut. When not in use the snare was sometimes placed behind the ear as one does a pencil. This saying is applied to one who will not heed—he uses his ears only to hold his snare" (Saying 2901). Shrimp-snaring, like eel-catching, was not considered an expert way of fishing. (Kamakau, *The Works* 59-60).

28. "The eyes thorny like lau hala" (maka kōkala lau hala): this phrase was used sometimes jestingly to refer to the people of Puna "who concealed the placenta of a new born child in a [hala] tree believing that the child's eyelashes would then grow long as the thorns on the hala leaves, thus giving the child a bright, keen look" (Pukui-Elbert *Hawaiian Dictionary*).

29. Kuapāka'a's insult here is also proverbial: "Kāhilihili lau 'ilima, A brushing off with 'ilima leaves." Pukui explains in *'Ōlelo No 'eau*: "After leaping into dirt at Kaumaea, Ka'ū, the players wiped off the dust that adhered to their skin with 'ilima branches before going to Paiaha'a to surf. Later applied to one who takes a sketchy bath" (Saying 1312). Kuapāka'a uses the word "kākā" "to beat off" rather than "kāhilihili" "to brush off."

30. Kā'ili: short for Kū-kā'ili-moku, a feathered war god passed on from Līloa to his son 'Umi to 'Umi's son Keawenuia'umi; both 'Umi and Keawenuia'umi called on its power in conquering the Big Island; it eventually belonged to Kamehameha, who conquered all the major islands except Kaua'i.

31. Kauwā: a caste, the lowest in the social order. "A people so despised that they were never allowed to mingle even with the commoners nor to marry anyone but a *kauwā*. Should any forbidden union take place and offspring result, the baby was put to death"; A kauwā could be used as a sacrificial victim if none other was available. Pukui speculates that the kauwā were early settlers in Hawai'i who were conquered by later settlers (Handy and Pukui 204-5). To be called a kauwā could be a grave insult in the class- and status-conscious ali'i society of ancient Hawai'i, though the term could be applied metaphorically to a servant, like Pāka'a, who humbly served his master, or to a worshiper of a god.

32. Ha'eha'e is at Kumukahi, the easternmost point of the Big Island, where the sun first appears in Hawai'i; Kumukahi is named for a hero from Kahiki

who landed there and is represented by a red stone; two wives in the form of stones, one named Ha'eha'e, manipulated the seasons by pushing the sun back and forth between them (i.e., from its northern position at the summer solstice to its southern position at the winter solstice.) These and many of the other place names in the chants can be identified with the help of *Place Names of Hawaii* (Pukui, Elbert, and Mookini) and located on the maps at the end of this text.

33. Kū, Lono, Kāne, and Kanaloa were the four major gods of ancient Hawai'i. Kū and Kāne were associated with the forests that provided the trees for building canoes; Lono was associated with rain and agriculture; Kāne and Kanaloa with spring water and fishing. Kū, in his manifestation as Kū'ula ("Red Kū"), was also a fishing god.

34. This chant is Pāka'a's greeting to Keawenuia'umi. Pāka'a was Keawenuia'umi's lawai'a, or fisherman; nehu was netted along shore and either eaten or used as bait for catching larger deep sea fish, such as aku, or bonito. Hilo was Keawenuia'umi's home district.

35. This chant contains a pun on *'ino,* meaning both "storm" and "wickedness." Thus, "the source of storms" also refers to "the source of wickedness," i.e., the two ho'okele who have usurped Pāka'a's positions in the royal court. The danger to Keawenuia'umi's life comes from both the real storm and the wickedness of the ho'okele who have misled him about Pāka'a. The same pun occurs in the following chants. This chant contains several place names of north and east Moloka'i (Kawaikapu, Waiehu, Kahiwa, Kikipua, Oloku'i, Wailau) and suggests a storm is coming from that direction. Malelewa'a could be a canoe landing ("Lele" means "to disembark"; "wa'a" is "canoe.")

36. The exact meaning of this chant and Nakuina's explication of it are unclear to the translator. Mahiki is a land division in Waimea, Hawai'i, where Hi'iaka, the sister of the volcano goddess Pele, destroyed a horde of mo'o (water lizards) called "mahiki." The trail through the region was apparently known for being wet and slippery from frequent rainfall. The demi-god Kamapua'a slipped and fell at Mahiki while chasing some supernatural bananas (Kahiolo 75-6). This chant referring to Mahiki seems to be a warning of the dangers at sea for the women on the canoe. The deck of a canoe gets wet and slippery when waves wash over it.

37. One of the navigator's duties was to read clouds and other sky elements for signs of good or bad weather for sailing. Kamakau says of Pāka'a: "He knew how to tell when the sea would be calm, when there would be a tempest in the ocean, and when there would be great billows. He observed the stars,

the rainbow colors at the edges of the stars, the way they twinkled, their red glowing, the dimming of the stars in a storm, the reddish rim on the clouds, the way in which they move, the lowering of the sky, the heavy cloudiness, the gales, the blowing of the *ho'olua* wind, the *a'e* wind from below, the whirlwind, and the towering billows of the ocean" *(Ruling Chiefs* 36). Pāka'a and his son not only read signs, they actually control the signs with their wind gourd and chants.

38. This chant gives the winds of the Big Island, clockwise, starting from Hilo. See the glossary of winds and rains of Hawai'i for the meanings of some of the wind names in this and other chants.

39. According to Handy and Handy, Ka 'Ilio a Lono ("The dog of Lono"), a large rock offshore of Ka Lae on the Big Island, is a dog turned to stone by Pele, the volcano goddess, because the dog joined the mo'o (water lizards) in an invasion of her lands. This rock is used to take bearings to locate offshore fishing grounds (248-9, 592). Kamakau gives a clearer explanation of the significance of this rock. One day, the dog of Lono went to drink at a freshwater spring in the ocean. The dog was turned to stone by Pele. The rock called Ka 'Ilio a Lono marks the location of this offshore underwater spring. When a kahuna told the ali'i Kalaniopu'u to go dig for the freshwater from this spring, theali'i's people couldn't find it and Kalaniopu'u put the kahuna to death *(Ruling Chiefs* 109-110). Beckwith notes that the freshwater spring is actually there in the ocean at Ka Lae and there are other underwater springs at Punalu'u, northeast of Ka Lae.

40. Hōkū'ula ("Red star"—the star Aldebaran?) and Hōkūlei ("Star wreath"— the star Capella?) were stars used for navigation.

41. One of the greatest fears of the ali'i was the desecration of their bones by fishermen who used human bones to make fishhooks. The mana (spiritual power) of a person resided in the bones, and this mana could be passed on to descendants only if the bones were taken care of. (Thus, Pāka'a carries the bones of his grandmother La'amaomao with him in his gourd.) Fishermen preferred the thigh bone and upper-arm bone for making hooks. If they were lucky enough to find a corpse at sea or washed ashore, they baked it in an imu and stripped off the flesh. Sometimes the flesh was used as bait to catch niuhi (tiger shark); or it could be left to scavengers, such as crabs and sea birds.

42. Harmful spirits: "pahulu pāo'o." Pahulu is the name of a king of harmful spirits who inhabited Lāna'i; these harmful spirits, called akua, killed and ate humans and had to be destroyed before fishermen could visit or humans could inhabit an area. According to Pukui-Elbert, "[Pahulu's] spirit could enchant fish." The pāo'o are goby fish that "love the rough seas and rocky coasts,

and love to leap from pool to pool"; one variety is displayed at the Bishop Museum with a note: "'vicious, kill off all trout'" (Titcomb 126).

43. According to Beckwith, the blackbird is a metaphor for a dark cloud; see her discussion of figurative language in Hawaiian literature in the introduction to *The Hawaiian Romance of Laieikawai*. "Ekeu-ekeu," the wind of Kaʻula is a variant of "'Ekekeu," or "wings." The Hawaiian islands were believed to be children of the gods ("given birth by Hina").

44. Pākaʻa's knowledge of fishing grounds and fishing is revealed in this chant, which also alludes to his plan to catch the two hoʻokele (whom he refers to as the uhu) with his carefully laid plot. The places named at the end of the chant are located along Molokaʻi's southeast and south-central coast, where Pākaʻa lived and fished.

45. Kaulua is a month, approx. February, in the six-month rainy season called Hoʻoilo, from November to April on the haole calendar. Kaulua may also be the name of a star (Sirius?) that marked the coming of this month in ancient times. (The Hawaiian months seem to have been marked by the appearances of stars at specific places and times in the sky.) The names of the months varied on each island and from island to island; in this story, the names are the ones commonly used on the Big Island (See Malo, 30-36).

46. The hīnālea (a wrasse) is Keawe, whom Pakaʻa is trying to tell to take shelter from the approaching storm. The angry uhu (parrot fish) are the Hoʻokeles, whom Pakaʻa is trying to lure into his trap. Coconut-fiber cords were used to lash the parts of a canoe together; the canoe creaked at sea, especially during a storm. This riddle-chant is based on a chant for Niu-ola-hiki, "Life-giving-coconut": "O life-giving coconut / That budded in Kahiki / That rooted in Kahiki / That formed a trunk in Kahiki / That bore leaves in Kahiki / That bore fruit in Kahiki / That ripened in Kahiki" ("The Legend of Niauepoʻo" in Pukui, *Hawaiian Folk Tales* 179-185). The sprouting coconut tree refers to Pākaʻa's plot, which will come to fruition in a storm at sea; Rubellite K. Johnson has suggested to Mrs. Mookini that the coconut tree is a metaphor for a waterspout. For a discussion of the important role of riddling in Hawaiian literature, see Martha W. Beckwith's "Hawaiian Riddling" in the *American Anthropologist,* Vol. 24, No. 3, July-September, 1922: "In some Hawaiian stories of the ancient past, the contest of wit is represented as one of the accomplishments of chiefs, taking its place with games of skill like arrow-throwing or checkers, with tests of strength like boxing or wrestling, and with the arts of war such as sling-stone and spear-throwing as a means of rivalry."

47. Welehu is approximately November, the first month in the six-month rainy season called Hoʻoilo (see note 45). Makaliʻi—about December;

Ka'elo—about January; Kaulua—about February; Nana—about March; Welo—about April; Ikiiki—about May.

48. Kulanihakoi is a mythical pond or lake in the sky; its overflow comes to earth as rain.

49. Kaluahole: possibly the southern coast of O'ahu between Waikīkī and Black Point; lit. "the pit of āhole, or white fish."

50. See note 47 for months of Ho'oilo, the rainy season.

51. According to Moke Manu ("Aiai, Son of Ku-ula," translated by Nakuina in Thrum's *Hawaiian Folk Tales*, 1907), 'Ai'ai, son of the fishing god Kū'ula, began this practice of kicking fish ashore when he saw mullet swarming near the beach at Kaunakakai. Hīlia is the coastal area of southern Moloka'i from Pākanaka fishpond to Kalama'ula.

52. Cf. "'*O ke aho pulu o ka Ho'oilo*'—Fishlines are wetted in Ho'oilo. Even if the waves rolled in continuously and there were heavy thunder and lightning and pouring rain, as long as there was no wind the fisherman had nothing to fear; only a storm that brought wind was dreaded" (Kamakau, *The Works* 77).

53. Kīauau: a shout used to encourage workers; translated "Hurry!"

54. "Hiki" means "to arrive"; Makaunulau (lit. "eyes drawing many") is the name of a navigation star, also called Kamakaunulau and Unulau. Unulau is also the name of a wind (Johnson and Mahelona, 9, 16, 21).

55. Kūapāka'a is punning on lā, which means both "sun" and "sail"; Kumukahi is the easternmost point of the Big Island, where the sun first appears in Hawai'i.

56. In the "Legend of Aukelenuiaiku," the hero saves his starving brothers on a long canoe voyage by opening one end of a magical club and providing food and water (Fornander, Vol. 4, 50). This allusion gives the historical character of Kūapāka'a a more heroic stature by associating him with a hero of ancient legend.

57. Saying No. 2706 in Mary Kawena Pukui's '*Ōlelo No'eau*: "*Pū'ali o Ka-hau-nui ia Ka-hau-iki.* Big-hau-tree has a groove worn into it by Little-hau-tree. Said when a child nearly wears out the patience of the adult in charge of him, or of a large company of warriors discomfited by a small one."

GLOSSARY

'ae: yes.

'ai: to eat; food; specifically vegetable food, like taro, sweet potatoes, poi, etc. as opposed to **i'a**, meat or fish.

'ai ahupua'a: ruler of an **ahupua'a**.

'āipu'upu'u: steward.

ahupua'a: a land division extending from the uplands to the sea.

aikāne punahele: "favorite friend," sometimes with homosexual connotations.

'ākōlea: fern with large, lacy fronds.

akua: god, gods.

'ākulikuli: a coastal herb.

ali'i: chief/chiefess; **ali'i 'aimoku:** ruler of or district or island [**moku**]; **ali'i loa** or **ali'i nui:** very high chief.

aloali'i: in the presence of chiefs, royal court.

aloha 'ino: What a pity!

'anae: mullet.

anana: distance between the tips of the longest fingers of a man with his arms extended on each side.

'ao: dried baked sweet potato; used as rations on voyages.

'a'ole: no.

'aumakua: family or personal god; pl.: **'aumākua**.

auwē : alas.

'awa: a shrub; the root was used to make a narcotic drink.

ē: say there! hey!; **ē ke keiki:** say there, child; **ē kēnā keiki:** hey, you child [**kēnā** is used disparagingly for "you"]; **ē nā keiki:** hey, you child [said disrespectfully sometimes].

'elele: messenger, envoy

haku: master, lord.

hala: pandanus tree; its leaves, with thorny edges stripped off, were woven into mats, baskets, and hats.

hale: a traditional house made from poles lashed together and thatched with pili grass; **hale 'āipu'upu'u**: house for provisions; **hale ho'opili wale**: to live as a dependent in someone else's house; to sponge off someone else.

hānai: provider.

hāpu'u: grouper (fish).

hau: a lowland tree; its soft, light wood was used for net floats and canoe outriggers; the sap and flowers were used medicinally; **hau iki**: a small hau tree; **hau nui**: a big hau tree.

he'e: squid.

heiau: place of worship.

hoewa'a: paddlers.

hīnālea: a brightly colored reef fish.

honu: turtle.

ho'okele or **ho'okele-wa'a**: canoe steersman-navigator.

ho'opili wale: to live as a dependent on others; to sponge; a person who lives in this way.

hulu manu: bird feathers.

i'a: meat, fish; **Ka I'a**: "The Fish"; the Hawaiian name for the Milky Way. **Ka I'a-lele-i-aka**, "The fish jumping in shadows" is the full phrase. **Ua huli Ka I'a** ("Ka I'a has turned") is glossed as "It's past midnight"; around April (Nana) the Milky Way is tilted up in the west and down in the east in the evening in the southern sky; moves parallel to the horizon at midnight; and tilts down in the west and up in the east after midnight.

ilāmuku: executive officer, marshall.

'ie: aerial roots of the 'ie'ie vine.

'ilima: native shrubs bearing yellow, orange, green, or dull red flowers; used for leis or to make a mild laxative.

'īlio: dog.

imu: cooking pit; an underground oven.

'ina: young sea urchin.

'iwa: frigate bird.

kā: exclamation of mild surprise, disapproval, or annoyance.

ka'au: forty.

kā-hā-hā: exclamation of surprise, wonder, or displeasure.

kāhala: amberjack.

kāhili: a feather standard symbolic of royalty.

kahu: honored attendant, guardian; **kahu iwikuamoʻo**: "backbone" attendant, the main personal attendant of an aliʻi.

kahuna: priest or expert; plural: **kāhuna.**

kākāʻōlelo: orator, adviser.

kālai-waʻa: canoe carver.

kalana: a division of land smaller than a **moku.**

kalo: taro.

kamaʻāina: "child of the land"; native born.

kanaka: human being; man; laborer, servant, attendant, retainer; this term designates common humanity, subjects of the aliʻi class, which claimed divine origin. pl: **kānaka; kanaka alualu aliʻi wale**: a person who runs after the aliʻi; **kanaka hoʻopili wale**: a person who lives off of another, wealthier person; **kanaka iki / kanaka nui** : unimportant person / important person; **kanaka kiʻekiʻe / kanaka haʻahaʻa**: elevated person / degraded person.

kapa: tapa made from tree bark; a tapa wrap or covering; **kapa kīhei**: tapa cape; **kapa māmaki**: tapa made from māmaki bark; **kapa paʻūpaʻū**: "moist tapa," layered tapa moistened during its making.

kapu: taboo; sacred.

Kau: the hot, dry season, beginning in Ikiiki, or about May and ending in Ikuwa, or about October. See notes 42 and 45.

kauhale: a group of houses, including men's and women's eating houses, sleeping house, cooking house, canoe house, etc.; cf. **hale.**

kāuna: four.

kauwā: a servant; an outcast.

keiki: child, offspring, boy, son; **keiki kauwā**: servant's child; **keiki makua**: full-grown offspring.

kil strologer.

kuhikuhipu'uone: soothsayer, seer, lit. "point-out the sand dunes," so called because he often advised in placing and building houses, temples, and fishponds.

Kuhina Nui: highest officer next to the king.

kukui: candlenut tree; its oily nut was burned in torches or chewed and spit on the ocean water to smooth the surface and increase the visibility into the depths.

Kū kū-'ai-moku! Lā-hai-na! 'O-i-a!: Ready! Set! Go!

kupuna: grandparent, ancestor; **kupunawahine**: grandmother; female ancestor.

lau hala: pandanus leaf; cf. **hala**.

lawai'a: fisherman; fishermen.

lehua: the flower of the '**ōhi'a** tree.

lei palaoa: whale-tooth pendant; a symbol of royalty; the ali'i made kapu whales washed ashore, so they could use the bones to make these highly prized ornaments.

lōpā: a peasant; shiftless, vagrant.

loulu: native palms; leaves used as umbrellas for protection from rain or sun.

luna kāhea official crier.

luna nui: head overseer.

mā: and company; and others; and associates.

mai'a: bananas

maka'āinana: commoners.

malihini: stranger, newcomer, guest, visitor; cf. **kama'āina**.

malo: loincloth.

mālolo: flying fish.

māmaki: small native tree; its bark was used to make tapa.

manini: surgeonfish.

manō: shark.

manu ka'upu: albatross

mauka: on land, this word means "toward the mountains"; at sea, it means "toward shore."

milo: a tree resembling the hau tree.

moa: chicken.

moi: threadfish.

moku: district.

muku: the length from fingertips of one hand to the elbow of the other arm when both arms are extended to the side.

na'ena'e: native daisy.

nehu: anchovy, eaten raw or dried, or used as bait to catch larger fish.

noio: noddy tern.

'ohana: family, kin group.

'ōhi'a: a native hard-wood tree with red flowers.

'ōhua: retainers, dependents, servants, members of a family, sojourners in a household.

olonā: a native shrub; the bark was twisted into a strong, durable cord.

'ōpae: shrimp.

'ōpakapaka: blue or grey snapper.

'ōpelu: mackerel scad.

'ope'ope: baggage, bundles.

pāhoe: to drive fish into a net by beating paddles rhythmically against the canoe; a person who performs this action.

pāki'i: flatfish.

pāo'o: a fish said to leap from pool to pool along the coast.

pelehū: a type of fish.

pili: a grass used for thatching.

po'e: people; **po'e ho'opili wale** or **po'e pipili wale**: people living off others; sponges; lit. "clinging people."

pōhuehue: beach morning glory.

pū kaua: generals, champions, war leaders.

pua'a: pig.

puhi: eel.

pū-loa: a species of octopus that comes out at night.

puna: a type of coral which washed ashore during storms.

pūpū: fish, chicken, or banana served with **'awa**.

pu'ukū: treasurer, steward.

kī: a woody plant, leaves used for capes and skirts or for wrapping food to be cooked in an imu.

'uala: sweet potato.

uhu: parrot fish.

ukana: baggage, cargo, supplies.

uku: deep-sea snapper.

'uku: louse, flea.

'ulae: lizard fish.

ulua: crevalle or jack (fish).

uoa: the false mullet.

wahahe'e: literally, "squid mouth" or "slippery mouth"; i.e. to lie, a lie, or a liar.

wahine: women; **wāhine**: women.

wai: fresh water.

wana: sea urchin.

WINDS AND RAINS OF HAWAI'I

(Compiled from the Pukui-Elbert *Hawaiian Dictionary*)

A'e / A'e-loa: the trade wind (Hāmākua, Hawai'i; Kala'au, Hawai'i; Lāwa'i, Kaua'i), cf. Kāpae, Kaomi, Moa'e.

'Āhiu: "wild, untamed"; a mountain wind (Kahana, O'ahu).

'Aiko'o: "canoe-eating" (Nu'alolo, Kaua'i).

'Ailoli: "sea-cucumber-eating" (Kaupō, Maui)

'Aimaunu: "bait-eating" (Hāna, Maui)

Ala'oli: a wind said to bring good weather (Hulē'ia, Kaua'i).

'Ao'aoa: a sea breeze at Honolulu.

'Āpa'apa'a: a strong wind (Kohala, Hawai'i).

'Awa: a cold mountain rain (Leleiwi, Hawai'i).

'Eka: a breeze that calls forth the canoes of Kona because it is good for fishing.

'E'elekoa: "stormy"; a storm wind (Uli, Hawai'i).

Hau: a cold, frosty breeze (Kapalilua, Hawai'i; Kula, Maui).

Haupe'epe'e: "to play hide and seek" (Kalihi, O'ahu).

Holokaomi: a wind at Paoma'i, Lāna'i.

Holopali: "running along the cliff" (Ka'a'awa and Kualoa, O'ahu).

Holopo'opo'o: "running in the hollow" (Waipi'o, Hawai'i).

Ho'olapa: "energetic, cavorting" (Ka'ū).

Ho'olua: a strong north wind (Hāna, Maui; Hālawa, Hala-nui, and Kaahakualua, Moloka'i; Makaīwa, Kaua'i).

Hulilua: "turning in two directions" (Hōmaikawa'a, Kaua'i).

Ihuanu: "cold nose"; a wind blowing from the uplands (Kawela, Moloka'i).

'Imihau: "dew-seeker"; a stormy wind of west Maui (Keka'a, Maui).

Inuwai: "water-drinking"; a sea breeze (Waipouli, Kaua'i).

Kā'ao: "to blow in gusts, with frequent lulls" (Hanamā'ulu, Kaua'i).

Ka'ele: a wind of Moloka'i (Pālā'au).

Kaiāulu: a pleasant, gentle trade wind of Maui (Pulupulu) and Oʻahu (Waiʻanae).

Kanilehua: "[rain that] lehua flowers drink" or "rain that makes lehua flowers rustle"; a misty rain of Hilo.

Kaomi: the northeast trade wind (Hāna, Maui); cf. Holokaomi

Kāpae: a trade wind (Hāna, Maui).

Kauaʻula: a strong, furious mountain wind associated with west Maui.

Kaʻula: a wind of Pōhakuloa, Maui.

Kaumuku: a rain squall (Papawai, Maui).

Kēhau: a gentle land breeze (Kona and Kapalilua, Hawaiʻi; Hālawa and Waialua, Molokaʻi; Waiopua and Kapo, Oʻahu; Ka-paʻa, Kauaʻi).

Kilihau: "cold shower" (Olowalu, Maui); cf. Hau.

Kiliua: a gentle, misty rain (Waikāne, Oʻahu).

Kiola-kapa: "kapa-tossing" (Kaelewaa, Molokaʻi).

Kipuʻupuʻu: a chilly wind and rain at Waimea Hawaiʻi.

Kiu: a strong, moderately cold wind from the northwest (cf. Kiuanu of Kalāheo, Kauaʻi, and Kiukainui of Koʻolau, Kauaʻi).

Koholā-lele ("leaping whale") / **Koholā-pehu** ("swollen whale"): a wind blowing from east to west (Hāmākua, Hawaiʻi; Kīpahulu, Maui).

Kololio: gust (Waikapū, Maui; Keōpuka, Molokaʻi; Moloaʻa, Kauaʼi).

Koʻomakani: a strong wind (Māhāʻulepū, Kauaʻi).

Kuehukai: "stirring up the sea" (Miloliʻi, Kauaʻi).

Kuehulepo: "stirring up dust" (Nāʻālehu, Hawaiʻi).

Kumumaʻomaʻo: an easterly wind (Kaluakoʻi, Molokaʻi; Kamaile, Oʻahu).

Lanikuʻuwaʻa: "heaven-releasing canoe" (Kalalau, Kauaʻi).

Lawakua: a mountain wind of Kauaʻi (Nāpali).

Lele-uli: "flying darkness," a gusty, gloomy wind; Ua lele-uli: a heavy wind-blown rain.

Līanu: "cool chill" (Hālawa, Molokaʻi).

Lūhau: "shaking down of dew or raindrops by a breeze" (Hanalei, Kauaʻi).

Lūpua: "to scatter flowers" (Wainiha, Kauaʻi).

124

Maheu: "to rake the earth" (Kalihi-wai, Kaua'i).

Malanai: a gentle breeze, the trade wind (Kailua, O'ahu; Kōloa, Kaua'i).

Mālua: a sea breeze, famous in song.

Mālualua: a north wind of O'ahu and Molokai.

Māunuunu: a strong, blustery wind (Wai'alae and Pu'uloa, O'ahu).

Mikioi: a gusty wind (Kawaihoa, Ni'ihau).

Moa'e: the trade wind (Kohala-iki, Hawai'i; Kahikinui, Maui; Pālā'au, Molokai; Punalu'u, O'ahu; Lehua island, west of Ni'ihau); cf. A'e.

Moani'ala: a wind, fragrant with the scent of hala, that wafts out to sea at Puna, Hawai'i.

Nāulu: a sudden shower; a showery wind (Kawaihae, Hawai'i; Kanaloa, Maui; Hālawa, Moloka'i; Ni'ihau).

'Ōlau-niu: "coconut-leaf-piercing" (Kekaha, Hawai'i; Kāhala and Kapālama, O'ahu).

Puahiohio: "whirlwind" (Nu'uanu, O'ahu).

Pu'ulena: a cold wind of Waiākea and Puna, Hawai'i.

Ua kea: "white rain" (Hilo, Hawai'i; also of Hāna, Maui).

'Ūkiu: a chilly north wind (Makawao, Maui)

'Ūkiukiu: diminutive of 'Ūkiu; a gentle breeze (Kalama'ula, Moloka'i).

'Ulalena: a reddish rain at Pi'iholo, Maui.

Ulumano: a strong, local wind blowing from a given direction (Puna, Hawai'i; Kāne'ohe, O'ahu)

Unulau: a wind famous in song; the trade wind; lit. "Pull-off-leaves."

Waiōpua: "water of cloud banks"; a gentle breeze (Wailua, Kaua'i).

Waipao: the cool breeze at Waimea, Kaua'i.

125

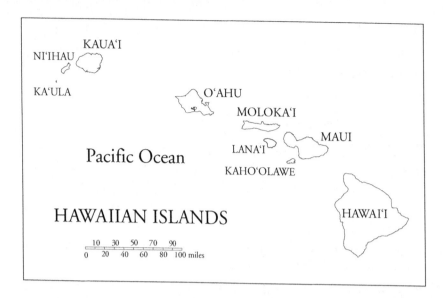

KAUA'I
NI'IHAU
KA'ULA

O'AHU
MOLOKA'I
MAUI
LANA'I
KAHO'OLAWE

Pacific Ocean

HAWAIIAN ISLANDS

HAWAI'I

10 30 50 70 90
0 20 40 60 80 100 miles

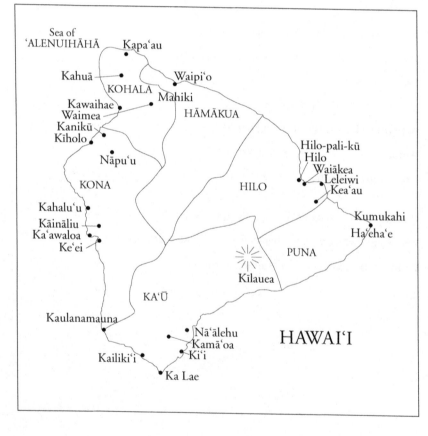

Sea of
'ALENUIHĀHĀ   Kapa'au

Kahuā
KOHALA   Waipi'o
Kawaihae   Mahiki
Waimea   HĀMĀKUA
Kanikū
Kīholo
Nāpu'u   Hilo-pali-kū
Hilo
Waiākea
KONA   Leleiwi
HILO   Kea'au
Kahalu'u
Kāināliu   Kumukahi
Ka'awaloa   Ha'eha'e
Ke'ei   PUNA
Kīlauea
KA'Ū
Kaulanamauna
Nā'ālehu   HAWAI'I
Kamā'oa
Kailiki'i   Ki'i
Ka Lae

126

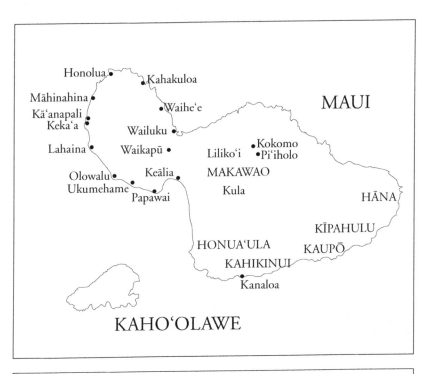

MAUI

Honolua
Kahakuloa
Māhinahina
Waiheʻe
Kāʻanapali
Kekaʻa
Wailuku
Lahaina
Waikapū
Likoʻi
Kokomo
Piʻiholo
Olowalu
Keālia
MAKAWAO
Ukumehame
Papawai
Kula
HĀNA

KĪPAHULU
HONUAʻULA
KAUPŌ
KAHIKINUI
Kanaloa

KAHOʻOLAWE

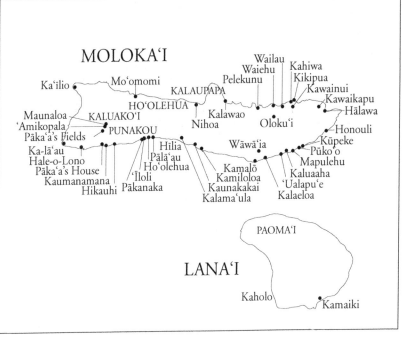

MOLOKAʻI

Wailau
Waiehu
Kahiwa
Kaʻilio
Moʻomomi
Pelekunu
Kikipua
KALAUPAPA
Kawainui
HOʻOLEHUA
Kawaikapu
Maunaloa
KALUAKOʻI
Kalawao
Hālawa
ʻAmikopala
Nihoa
Olokuʻi
Pākaʻaʻs Fields
PUNAKOU
Honouli
Ka-lā-au
Hīlia
Wāwāʻia
Kūpeke
Hale-o-Lono
Pālāʻau
Pūkoʻo
Pākaʻaʻs House
Hoʻolehua
Mapulehu
Kaumanamana
ʻĪloli
Kamalō
Kaluaaha
Hikauhi
Pākanaka
Kamiloloa
ʻUalapuʻe
Kaunakakai
Kalaeloa
Kalamaʻula

PAOMAʻI

LANAʻI

Kaholo
Kamaiki

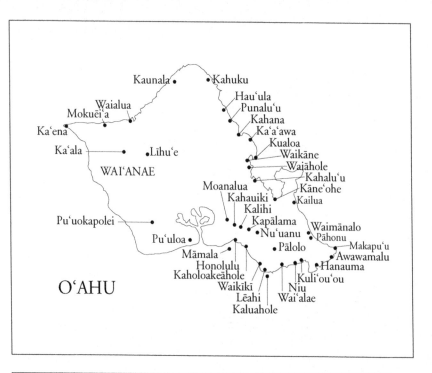

O'AHU

Kaunala
Kahuku
Hau'ula
Waialua
Punalu'u
Mokuei'a
Kahana
Ka'ena
Ka'a'awa
Ka'ala
Līhu'e
Kualoa
Waikāne
WAI'ANAE
Waiāhole
Kahalu'u
Moanalua
Kāne'ohe
Kahauiki
Kailua
Kalihi
Pu'uokapolei
Kapālama
Waimānalo
Pu'uloa
Nu'uanu
Pāhonu
Pālolo
Makapu'u
Māmala
Awawamalu
Honolulu
Hanauma
Kaholoakeāhole
Kuli'ou'ou
Waikīkī
Niu
Lēahi
Wai'alae
Kaluahole

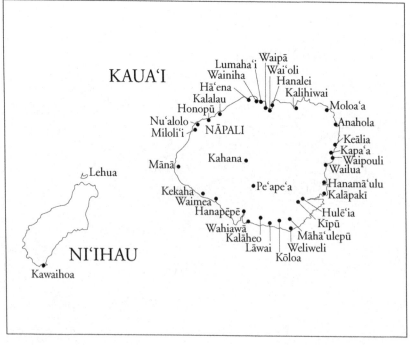

KAUA'I

Waipā
Lumaha'i
Wai'oli
Wainiha
Hanalei
Hā'ena
Kalihiwai
Kalalau
Honopū
Moloa'a
Nu'alolo
Anahola
Miloli'i
NĀPALI
Keālia
Kapa'a
Kahana
Waipouli
Mānā
Wailua
Pe'ape'a
Hanamā'ulu
Kekaha
Kalāpakī
Waimea
Hanapēpē
Hulē'ia
Wahiawā
Kīpū
Kalāheo
Māhā'ulepū
Lāwai
Weliweli
Kōloa

Lehua

NI'IHAU

Kawaihoa

REFERENCES

Beckley, Emma Metcalf. "Hawaiian Fisheries and Methods of Fishing with an Account of The Fishing Implements used by The Natives of the Hawaiian Islands." Honolulu: Advertiser Steam Print, 1883).

Beckwith, Martha W.*The Hawaiian Romance of Laieikawai with Introduction and Translation by Martha W. Beckwith.* In the *Thirty -third Annual Report of the Bureau of American Ethnology.* Washington, 1919.

Fornander, Abraham.*Hawaiian Antiquities and Folk-lore,* Vol. 4 and 5. Honolulu: Bishop Museum, 1918.

Handy, E.S. Craighill, and Elizabeth Green Handy. *Native Planters in Old Hawaii: Their Life, Lore, and Environment.* Honolulu: Bishop Museum, 1972.

Handy, E.S. Craighill, and Mary Kawena Pukui. *The Polynesian Family System in Ka'-u, Hawaii'i.* Rutland, VT: Tuttle, 1972.

Ii, John Papa. *Fragments of Hawaiian History.* Honolulu: Bishop Museum, 1959.

Johnson, Rubellite Kawena, and John Kaipo Mahelona. *Nā Inoa Hōkū: A catalogue of Hawaiian and Pacific Star Names.* Honolulu: Topgallant, 1975.

Kahiolo, G.W. *He Moolelo No Kamapuaa/The Story of Kamapuaa.* Trans. by Esther T. Mookini and Erin C. Neizmen with David Tom. Honolulu: Hawaiian Studies Program, 1978.

Kalakaua, David. *The Legends and Myths of Hawaii: The Fables and Folk-Lore of a Strange People.* Rutland, Vermont: Charles E. Tuttle, 1972. (Originally published in 1888.)

Kamakau, Samuel M. *The People of Old.* Honolulu: Bishop Museum, 1964.

Kamakau, Samuel M. *Ruling Chiefs of Hawaii.* Honolulu: Kamehameha Schools, 1961.

Kamakau, Samuel M. *The Works of the People of Old.* Honolulu: Bishop Museum, 1976.

Lewis, David. *We, the Navigators.* Honolulu: UH Press, 1973.

Makemson, Maud W. *The Morning Star Rises.* New Haven: Yale University Press 1941.

Malo, David, *Hawaiian Antiquities.* Honolulu: Bishop Museum, 1951.

Pukui, Mary Kawena. *Hawaiian Folk Tales.* Poughkeepsie: Vassar, 1933.

Pukui, Mary Kawena. *'Ōlelo No'eau: Hawaiian Proverbs and Poetical Sayings.* Honolulu: Bishop Museum, 1983.

Pukui, Mary Kawena, Samuel H. Elbert, and Esther T. Mookini. *Place Names of Hawaii.* Honolulu: UH Press, 1974.

Pukui, Mary Kawena, and Samuel H. Elbert *Hawaiian Dictionary.* Honolulu: UH Press, 1971.

Thrum, Thomas G. *Hawaiian Folk Tales, a Collection of Native Legends.* Chicago: A.C. McClurg and Co., 1907.

Titcomb, Margaret. *Native Use of Fish in Hawaii.* Honolulu: UH Press, 1972.

Westervelt, William D. *Hawaiian Legends of Old Honolulu.* Rutland, VT: Charles E. Tuttle, 1963.

41370720R00086

Made in the USA
Middletown, DE
05 April 2019